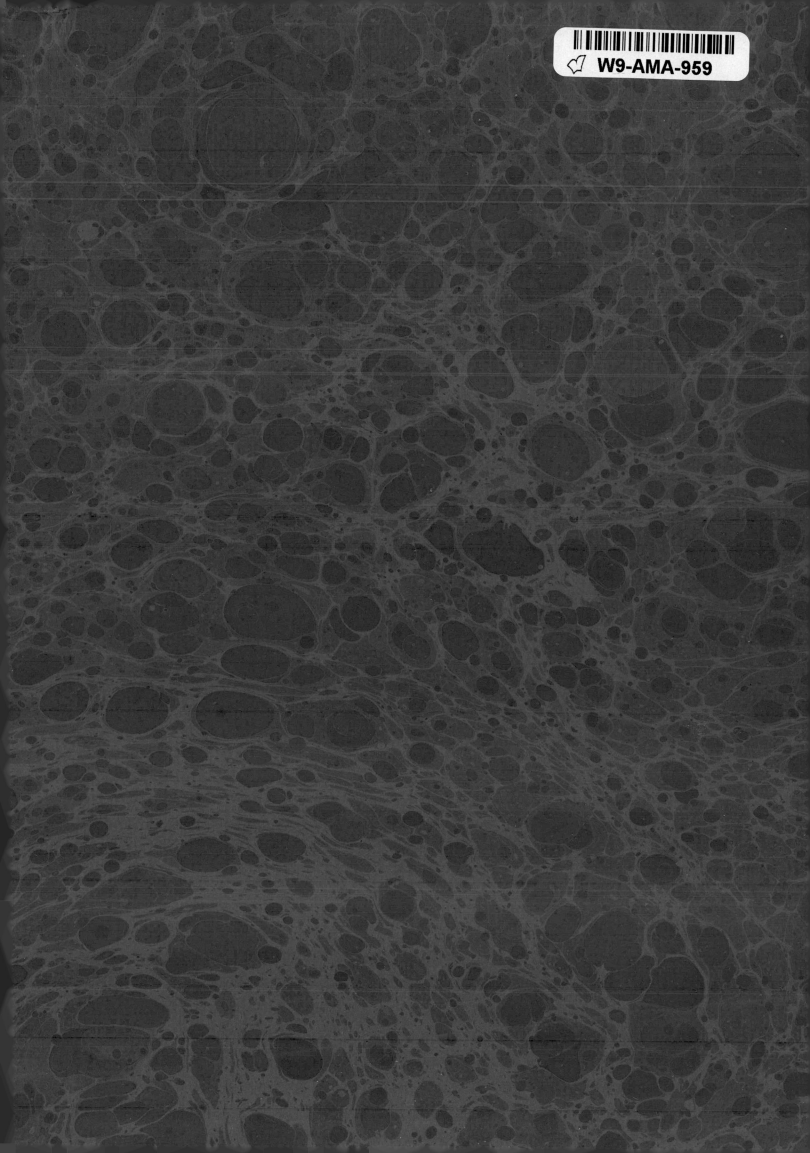

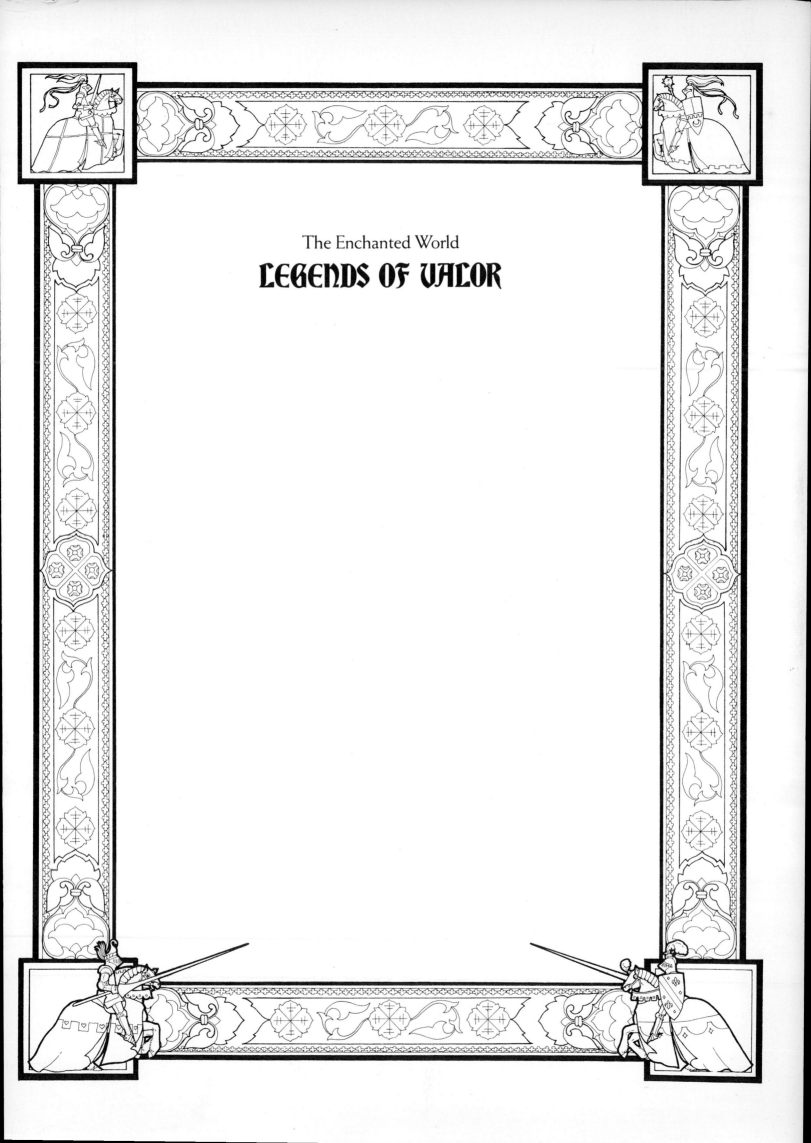

The Enchanted World

# LEGENDS OF VALOR

The Enchanted World

# LEGENDS OF VALOR

by Brendan Lehane
and the Editors of Time-Life Books

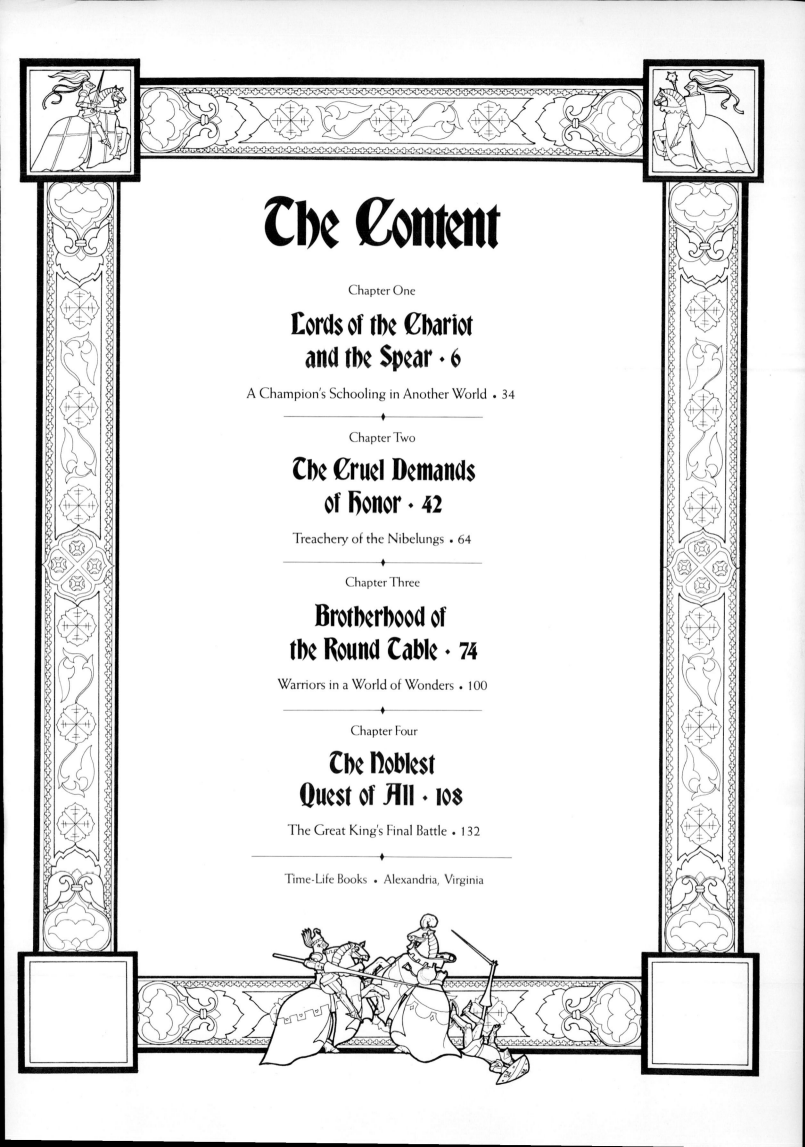

# The Content

Time-Life Books · Alexandria, Virginia

# Chapter One

# Lords of the Chariot and the Spear

In the days of Ireland's glories, when the island was divided into five warring kingdoms and the jet black ravens of the battle goddess wheeled above the shield-shaped hills, there came to his prime a warrior named Cuchulain. As it was for all warriors in those days, youth was a time of testing, and the tests he faced were many and harsh.

Cuchulain was a Red Branch knight—one of a warrior band whose title derived from the fact that the men served Conchobar of Ulster, a King descended from Ross the Red. The young men of Conchobar's cadre were like most Celts of that time—brilliant and fearless in battle, united as brothers against Conchobar's foes and quarrelsome as fighting cocks among themselves. The current fraternal dispute had dragged on for months, while Ulster remained at uneasy peace with its neighbors. The three finest of the Red Branch knights could not agree on who was the proven champion of the realm, and close though they were, the rivalry for that signal honor divided them.

Not wishing to court enmity by choosing one man

To determine the greatest of Ulster's warriors, a giant proposed a test: He would
allow the men to behead him if he could return the blow. The giant, unlike
the men, could pick up his severed head and walk away alive.

above another, Conchobar had sent the three for judgment to the Queen of Connacht in the west and the King of Munster in the south. But the judgment of the Queen satisfied no one, and the King of Munster—a man of magic, always elusive—could not be found. On Conchobar's orders a truce prevailed among the three knights: Loegaire the Triumphant, Conall of the Victories and Cuchulain. But it was a sullen truce.

That was the situation one winter's evening at the House of the Red Branch in Conchobar's hill fort of Emain Macha. Conchobar had invited his warriors to a night of feasting while the bitter winter winds howled outside. But only Loegaire happened to be in the hall. The three contentious champions now spent little time in one another's company; Conchobar had forbidden fighting, and they could not be sure of their tempers.

Amid the shouting and the boasting, the genial abuse and applause, the barking of excited hounds, nobody noticed the latch of the timbered door rise from its socket. Nobody saw or heard the door swing on greased hinges massively riveted into solid oak. But the wall-shaking slam it made as it crashed home silenced the company. Suddenly alert, the knights turned toward the door.

There, eyes glowing like flames, stood a gigantic man. Like canopies of rock, his forehead and nose threw shadows on the pocked and dusty limestone of his cheeks, more than half of which lay hidden beneath a broom of black and bristly beard.

His loins were swathed in cowhide and his shoulders in a cloak of matted wool. In one massive fist he carried a log as easily as ordinary men carried clubs of Derry oak. In the other rested an ax.

Slowly, each footstep reverberating against the roof beams, the figure strode to the hearth. Waves of his body heat enveloped those he passed. All heads turned with his progress, but nobody spoke. The terrified dogs, tails turned under their bellies, backed quickly away at the giant's approach. He planted the columns of his legs in front of the blazing logs and he threw down his own log. From under black brows he surveyed the warriors and silently challenged them to speak.

None did, and at length the giant spoke. His name, he said, was Uath the Stranger, and he roamed the world, searching for a man who could hold fast to his word. "Surely here in the House of the Red Branch," he said, "sits one who will make a compact with me and keep it."

Then Fergus Mac Roy, kinsman of Conchobar the King, spoke for the company. "And what is this compact?" said Fergus.

"Easy to tell," replied Uath the Stranger. "You and Conchobar I put aside, because you are Kings. Outside of you, I seek one who will make this bargain: He to strike off my head tonight and I to return the same blow tomorrow night. Surely here there is one whose courage can meet the terms."

The answer he got was silence, for the terms were surpassingly odd ones, and smelled of magic. No knight stepped forward. "There is, then, no champion here," said the giant and smiled a wintry smile.

"Here is one who braves your challenge,

8

clown," cried a voice, and Loegaire the Triumphant leaped to the center of the hall.

"Kneel, then," he said to the giant. "I give you my word: I cut off your head tonight, you cut off mine tomorrow."

Uath knelt and laid his head upon the log. With a mighty effort, Loegaire raised the giant's ax high. Down came the blade, whistling its death song. It struck through the giant's neck, and the creature's head lolled and then thumped onto the flagstones of the floor. Great gouts of blood spurted from the trunk.

Speechless and white-faced, Loegaire stepped back and stared. For after an instant, the body rose to its feet, the lack of a head making no difference to its steadiness and poise. It took the ax from Loegaire's nerveless hands; it picked up the head, clutching the hair to its chest so that blood trickled in scarlet rivulets down to its legs. The face looked outward, as glowering and disdainful as when it had first appeared. Gripping its blood-soaked baggage, the massive figure marched to the doorway and then out into the night.

The next night, as before, the door of the House of the Red Branch swung open, letting in the wind and rain. Uath the Stranger—whole again, without so much as a mark on his sinewy neck—strode to the hearth, bearing his ax. His glowing eyes ranged across the company of knights.

Loegaire the Triumphant was not in attendance. His otherwise great heart had failed him at the prospect of accepting the giant's terrible blow. Uath shrugged and spat on the floor. He fingered the ax blade and said not a word.

From the crowded benches sprang Con-

all of the Victories, ready to defend Ulster's honor. The same murderous compact was struck: a head for a head. As Loegaire had, Conall swung the ax; the blood of Uath the Stranger spurted as before. As before, the headless giant left the feasting hall. And as before, the Ulsterman was absent on the next night, when it came his turn to brave the blade.

In the flickering firelight stood Uath the Stranger, and he laughed at the weak-willed Ulster knights. "Two of the best have failed me," said he. "And where is the proud stripling Cuchulain? Lily-hearted, like the rest."

Then Cuchulain rose from the bench where he sat that night. He spoke coolly enough. He told the giant to keep his bargain for fools. Why, he asked, would a sensible man throw his life away for the sake of beheading a creature that could restore its devil's form by trickery? The giant bellowed with laughter. He called Cuchulain coward and spineless child.

The taunts did the trick. Crimson with pride and rage, Cuchulain sprang from his bench to the center of the hall; strong in fury, he snatched the ax and swung it, sending Uath's head spinning in bloody arcs to the rafters. When the head fell, Cuchulain smashed it with the edge of the ax. Then there was silence, save for the young knight's heavy breathing.

As before, the giant rose, picked up his ax and the reddened pulp that had been his head, and strode out into the darkness.

The following night found Cuchulain at his usual place in the hall. He was tight-

lipped and white-faced, but he was there.

The Red Branch knights drew back from him, as from one marked for death. On his raised bench, Conchobar the King – with Fergus beside him – waited impassively.

The door swung open and the faces turned toward it. Uath strode in once more. He called Cuchulain's name.

Cuchulain walked stiffly to the center of the hall and knelt to take the blow. His head trembled. His pale face glistened with the sweat of fear, but he kept his place while the giant towered over him.

The ax swung up – its blade silvered by the firelight – and paused in the air.

"Stretch out your neck better," the giant commanded.

"Save your breath and cease your taunting," Cuchulain snapped. "Strike swiftly, as I did." He bent his head again.

The giant's eyes gleamed as the ax hurtled down. A hoarse gasp left a hundred throats, the beginning of the Red Branch's mourning for the loss of its own.

But there was no loss. The giant's ax blade shattered the stones on which Cuchulain knelt. The young warrior himself rose to his feet unharmed and turned to face Uath the Stranger.

Uath had disappeared. In his place stood Curoi of Munster – that kingdom of magical mists and mountains far to the south of Ulster – he who had been so strangely absent when the rival knights presented themselves for his judgment. Curoi had come at Conchobar's asking to settle the quarrel of the Ulster champions in full view of their peers, so that none would doubt the fairness of his decision. The King of Munster spoke then:

He told the company that Cuchulain was the King's champion. Only Cuchulain had refused the fool's bargain; Loegaire and Conall had accepted it, then failed in valor. Only Cuchulain had struck in the heat of rage – a rashness appropriate and even necessary to a warrior. Only Cuchulain had proved his contempt of death by bending his head for the giant's blow.

In that uncertain age, it mattered that the question of the champion's precedence have an answer. It was not only for the honor of the thing that the Ulstermen named champions. So long as the question of valor remained open, there was division and quarreling in the king's hall, and Ulster stayed weak from squabbling with itself. No one disputed the king's authority – kings were born with that – but standing alongside the king there had to be his champion, his hero. If the king symbolized the land itself and all of its people, his heroic champion stood for their warrior spirit and fought for them in battle. The hierarchy of bravery had to be established and acknowledged as well as the hierarchy of state. A tribe without a hero was a piteous and vulnerable thing.

For in the earliest age of heroes, order was fragile, and the boundaries between nations were as fluid as the rivers that marked the clearest and most defensible of them. Tribes moved massively across Europe like herds of animals, searching for forage and shelter and for other, weaker tribes, whose wealth could be taken and whose people enslaved. Migration seemed endless, and warfare and feuding

11

were an almost permanent state of affairs.

This was so for centuries: Civilization and order advanced, but they advanced slowly, and for defense they depended on the strong arms of the valiant. From Cuchulain's time, when Celtic warriors fought from chariots, relying for protection on leather shields, to the age of King Arthur, when armored men fought on horseback, every kingdom needed champions. These were the greatest and most valorous of the warriors who fought the king's battles for him and sat in high places in his hall; these heroes were the diamonds that sparkled in his crown.

Their bright valor still shines across the years. Indeed, they conducted their lives so that their names might breathe forever in the words of poets and all others who cherish bravery. And their deeds were not forgotten—the storytellers sang for centuries the legends of the brave. They told of Cuchulain and the Red Branch knights and of a later Irish hero, Finn Mac Cumal, with his band of warriors ever guarding the Irish shore against invaders. Scandinavian bards immortalized Bothvar Bjarki, who wielded his magical sword in the service of the King of Denmark; and Sigurd the Volsung fought beside the Germanic Nibelungs. In the more rarefied light of a later age came Arthur of Britain and the knights of the Round Table—Lancelot and Gawain, Percival and Bors, Tristram and the matchless Galahad.

The most renowned of them were not as other mortals. They were braver, it is true, but the greatest heroes were also in some

way innately different, more closely linked than their fellows to the other world, where magic reigned. Their mothers were often mortal princesses—it was not given to the daughters of peasants to bring forth heroes. But the women conceived in curious ways, and people whispered that the gods or members of the fairy race brought about the conceptions.

Thus in the Aegean lands, the hero Perseus was said to have been fathered by Zeus, who appeared to Perseus' mother, Danae, in a shower of gold. And indeed, Perseus had supernatural help throughout his adventures; even his accouterments were enchanted, so that he had the powers of both flight and invisibility (page 15). In later times and other places, similar stories were told. It was said that the Volsung—the grandfather of the hero Sigurd—had in him the blood of the war god Odin. And as for Cuchulain, the poets sang that his father was the Irish sun god, Lugh.

At any event, Cuchulain's birth was certainly mysterious. Cuchulain's mother, according to one version of the tale, was Dechtire, sister of King Conchobar. On the day she married a lord called Sualtim, Dechtire drank a cup of wine; a mayfly flew into the cup and she swallowed it. She fell then into a deep sleep, and in her dream, the sun god, Lugh, appeared. Lugh said that he had taken the mayfly's form in order to enter her, and he summoned her away, whereupon Dechtire and her maidens took the shape of beautiful birds linked each to the other by chains of gold and silver. This dazzling flock flew far from Emain Macha and sheltered, it was said, in the underground world of the Side – the fairy race of Ireland.

Nothing was heard of Dechtire for a full year. Then a flock of birds appeared at Emain Macha and led Conchobar and his knights to a palace in the south of Ulster. In the palace the King found his sister; she had given birth to a son – he who would one day be called Cuchulain – and she told the King of her dream. The King gave the infant the name of Setanta and, for courtesy's sake, the title Son of Sualtim to spare the pride of Dechtire's husband. Then Conchobar left the child secluded in his mother's keeping, far from the royal fortress at Emain Macha, until he should reach the age for warrior's training.

Or so the storytellers said. And indeed, the adventures of Cuchulain's short life revealed that like other heroes he had links with a world beyond the fields and farms and fortresses that formed the landscapes of ordinary men.

In the young age of creation, the divisions between the familiar world of humankind and other dimensions were ever shifting. The ordered universe of tree and rock and cloud, where the hours marched in measured pace marked by the progress of the sun, was open to magic and to strange beings ruled by patterns no mortals understood.

The boundaries of the other worlds were elusive and always changeable: Any form of divider or border line in the mortal world might at some point prove a portal to the realm of wonders. An ordinary gate in a wall might open every day but one onto an ordinary meadow, grazed by placid sheep. On a certain day, however, the open gate might reveal a white-capped sea, stretching to infinity and dotted with islands where monsters lived, or a rolling plain where silent warriors marched.

Every day but one, an Irish hill might present a bland and grassy flank to those who toiled in the fields around it, but on the night of that one day, the hillside might open wide to reveal another, twilight land within, crowded with the shining beings of the Side, who dwelt, as was well known, within the hollow hills. Such a hill was found in Connacht. That was the mound at Cruachan, where the warrior Queen Maeve had her fortress. On the night of Samain, the Celtic night of the dead, which marked the division between summer and winter, strange creatures issued from that mound. Goblins crawled forth, along with scarlet birds and three-headed vultures. Ordinary folk stayed close to home then, having no wish to encounter the inimical beings hidden beyond the borders of their lives.

But it was the fate of heroes, extraordinary themselves, to cross the boundaries of the ordinary. That fate was clear not only from the circumstances of the heroes' births but also from the patterns of their childhoods. Destined for strange ventures, young heroes like Cuchulain were hidden away and sedulously protected while they were vulnerable. Thus the young hero Finn Mac Cumal was kept throughout his childhood from the sight of the warriors of Ireland – particularly those who had killed his father and usurped Finn's rightful inheritance; Finn's

son, Oisin, was reared in a secluded mountain glen by a deer (*page 8*). Much later, Merlin the Enchanter — who by magic had arranged the conception of King Arthur — hid the boy Arthur until he was ready to assume his kingdom.

When the time was ripe and the youths were ready, they came forth from their seclusion to join the warriors' world and receive their training, their arms, their adult names — given for the qualities they displayed — and their rightful places. They generally were amazingly young when this occurred: Cuchulain was only seven and still bore his child's name, Setanta, when he left his mother's house. It happened that during his childhood he heard much of the court at Emain Macha. He heard descriptions of the fortress, of the warriors of the Red Branch, of the boys in training to join that splendid company and of King Conchobar. Of the King bards sang: "In form and shape and dress, in size and straightness and symmetry, in eye and hair and whiteness, in wisdom and skill and speech, in garments and splendor and array, in weapons and amplitude and dignity, in manners and feats of arms and descent, there was not on earth the figure of a man like the figure of Conchobar."

And fired by this lofty vision of the King — who was, after all, his uncle — Setanta grew restless. His toy weapons were nothing to him now. He demanded his mother Dechtire's leave to go to Emain Macha, but she only smiled and said that he was too young and the way too far. She told him that when a proper and well-born traveler passed, she would put Setanta in his care so that the boy would have a sponsor in seeking admission to the court.

But the impetuous Setanta would not wait. He learned the direction in which Emain Macha lay, and set off alone to seek his fortune, carrying nothing but his miniature javelin and his hurling stick and ball. The stick and ball were the implements of a field game that resembled hockey and was favored as a sport for fledgling warriors because the strokes strengthened the muscles and developed balance and dexterity. But Setanta's skills were already surpassing. It was later said that as he trod the long miles across the Ulster moors and through the forests, he amused himself by throwing ball, stick and javelin ahead of him, then running to catch them all before they could fall to the ground.

Whether or not that was true, it was certainly true that the boy conducted himself valiantly. Little attention was paid to the seven-year-old as he passed through Conchobar's fortress gates. He wandered among lounging soldiers and serving people until he found the field by the thatched Boys' House, where the children of the court were trained.

Shouting in deafening chorus, a crowd of boys battled at hurling on the muddy field. Without a moment's hesitation, Setanta sprang among the players and captured the ball; wiry and agile, he darted through the crowd and drove the ball home. He then turned at the goal and faced a cluster of larger children.

"Common," said one. "Ill-behaved," said another. "The stranger has no right to join us." Fists clenched, the children

## A gift of magic weaponry

Heroes were human and yet greater than human. They dared to venture beyond the mortal world and, in their daring, often found more than mortal aid. This was so in the north, where Irish heroes lived and fought. And it was true as well in the sunny isles of Greece, where once lived Perseus, a warrior who was given a frightful task by a King who wished him dead.

Perseus' mission was to take the head of Medusa. But this was manifestly impossible, for Medusa was a Gorgon, a winged monster whose very appearance turned men to stone.

Magic furnished Perseus with the tools to complete the quest. Athena, the goddess of wisdom, lent him her polished shield; Hermes, the messenger of the gods, gave him a sword. But more than that, Hermes took the young warrior to the land at the back of the North Wind, where nymphs armed him with enchantments: They gave Perseus winged sandals with which he could fly, a wallet that could hold whatever was put in it and a helmet of invisibility.

So, buoyed like a bird and transparent as the wind, Perseus found the Gorgons where they laired. Wings folded, hair a mass of seething snakes, the creatures slept. Perseus did not look at them. He watched their reflections in his shield and, thus guided, beheaded Medusa where she lay among her sisters.

With the head safely hidden in his wallet, he flew to his home island. There he found the King among his courtiers, and Perseus had his revenge. He drew the head from the wallet and held it before the King's face. Even in death the Gorgon magic worked. The King was rendered into stone where he stood.

advanced upon Setanta. A few threw their hurling sticks straight at the intruder.

Setanta dodged and charged his tormentors. Howling with fury, he dashed in among the older boys, kicking and punching, biting and scratching. One by one, he brought them down and smashed their smug faces into the mud — until the uproar drew the attention of a king's man and the fight was stopped. The older boys were set to training exercises under the stern eye of a man-at-arms. Setanta, the collar of his tunic held firmly in a large fist, was taken to Conchobar. The child's fierce courage made an impression on the King. In a quiet, kindly voice, Conchobar asked Setanta whence and from whom he had come.

When Conchobar learned Setanta's name and family, he welcomed the child as his own and sent him to join the boys' troop, where the children worked out their differences in the rough-and-ready fashion that children have always used. Conchobar, however, recalled a prediction made at Setanta's birth — that he would be praised by chariot drivers and fighters and loved by all, that he would avenge the King's wrongs and defend the King's fords and fight the King's battles. Conchobar therefore provided the boy with the best of foster fathers as teachers: Sencha, chief judge of Ulster; Amergin the poet; Blai the lord marshal of the troops; and Fergus, kinsman and chief adviser to the King. They loved the boy and taught him well.

For some time, the boy Setanta's life passed like that of any other royal child. He spent his days at Emain Macha, practicing with spear, javelin, sword and short sword; with battle-ax and sling; with bow and arrow. The boys learned the ways of horses and the handling of teams. The Celts of that time fought from two-wheeled chariots — and with such skill that they awed the enemies who fought them, including such sophisticated commanders as Julius Caesar, who once wrote: "By daily training and practice, they attain such proficiency that even on a steep incline they are able to control the horses at full gallop, and to check and turn them in a moment. They can run along the chariot pole, stand on the yoke and get back into the chariot as quick as lightning."

The child Setanta grew strong and skillful. Sooner than the others, he acquired his man's name and the arms of a man, showing the spirit that made a man a warrior of the first rank.

His man's name derived from his own actions. In those days, smiths — the forgers of weapons — were revered by king and commoner alike, so when Culann, the most famous of Ulster smiths, invited King Conchobar to feast with him, the King accepted gladly. He summoned Setanta, the pride of his fledglings, to join him as soon as the day's training was done.

When the afternoon light began to slant across the playing field and the boys returned to their quarters, Setanta set off for the smith's house, following the track of the King's chariots. He walked for an hour or so, throwing a golden hurling ball ahead of him as was his habit, and at last came upon the high stockade that fortified the house of Culann the smith.

The gate was shut and barred with iron. Forgetting that the boy was coming, Culann had called the (continued on page 21)

# A Lineage of Enchantment

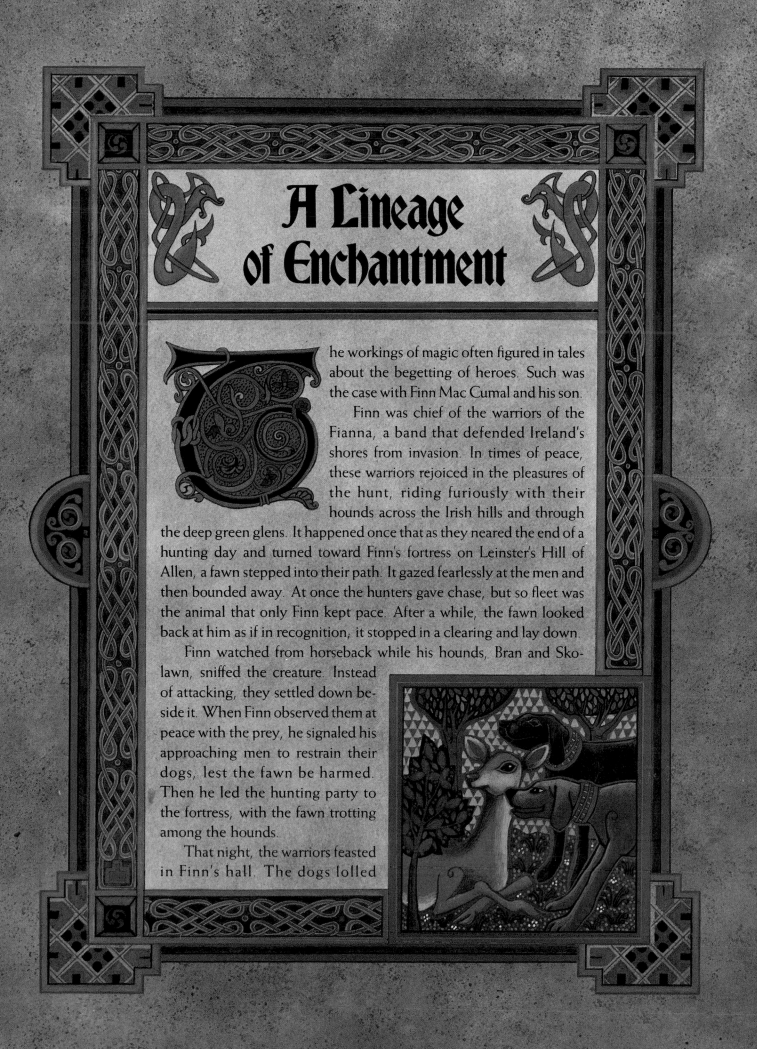

The workings of magic often figured in tales about the begetting of heroes. Such was the case with Finn Mac Cumal and his son.

Finn was chief of the warriors of the Fianna, a band that defended Ireland's shores from invasion. In times of peace, these warriors rejoiced in the pleasures of the hunt, riding furiously with their hounds across the Irish hills and through the deep green glens. It happened once that as they neared the end of a hunting day and turned toward Finn's fortress on Leinster's Hill of Allen, a fawn stepped into their path. It gazed fearlessly at the men and then bounded away. At once the hunters gave chase, but so fleet was the animal that only Finn kept pace. After a while, the fawn looked back at him as if in recognition; it stopped in a clearing and lay down.

Finn watched from horseback while his hounds, Bran and Sko-lawn, sniffed the creature. Instead of attacking, they settled down beside it. When Finn observed them at peace with the prey, he signaled his approaching men to restrain their dogs, lest the fawn be harmed. Then he led the hunting party to the fortress, with the fawn trotting among the hounds.

That night, the warriors feasted in Finn's hall. The dogs lolled around them, snuffling for scraps on the floor, and the fawn wandered freely, watching Finn with soft brown eyes. At last, when the torches guttered and the men settled down to sleep, the creature picked its way through the dogs to Finn's side. He smiled at it, and when he did so, the fawn vanished.

In its place stood a woman as fair as a flower. She spoke in a voice like the whispering of the wind, explaining to Finn that she was a woman of the fairy folk from the other world hidden beneath the Irish hills. She had been changed into fawn shape by a wizard of the fairy folk whose love she had spurned. The man had made her a beast, speechless and vulnerable. He had imprisoned her and used her so cruelly that one of his own slaves took pity and told her to take refuge with Finn, whose fortress was proof against the wizard's spells.

Finn listened and loved her, and that same night she gave herself to him. Then he found he could not bear to leave her side. Since she could not venture from the safety of the fortress, he stayed with her.

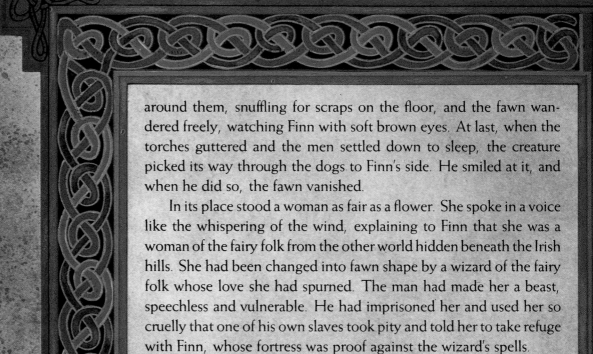

Such was his love that, against all custom, he ceased to hunt and fight. The warriors grumbled, but Finn, lost in love, heard nothing, or if he heard, paid no heed.

The day came, however, when Finn had to leave his bride. Invaders threatened the Irish shore, and honor demanded that he lead the Fianna to battle. His wife stayed behind, safe in his fortress on the Hill of Allen.

Or so he fondly thought. When, seven days later, he

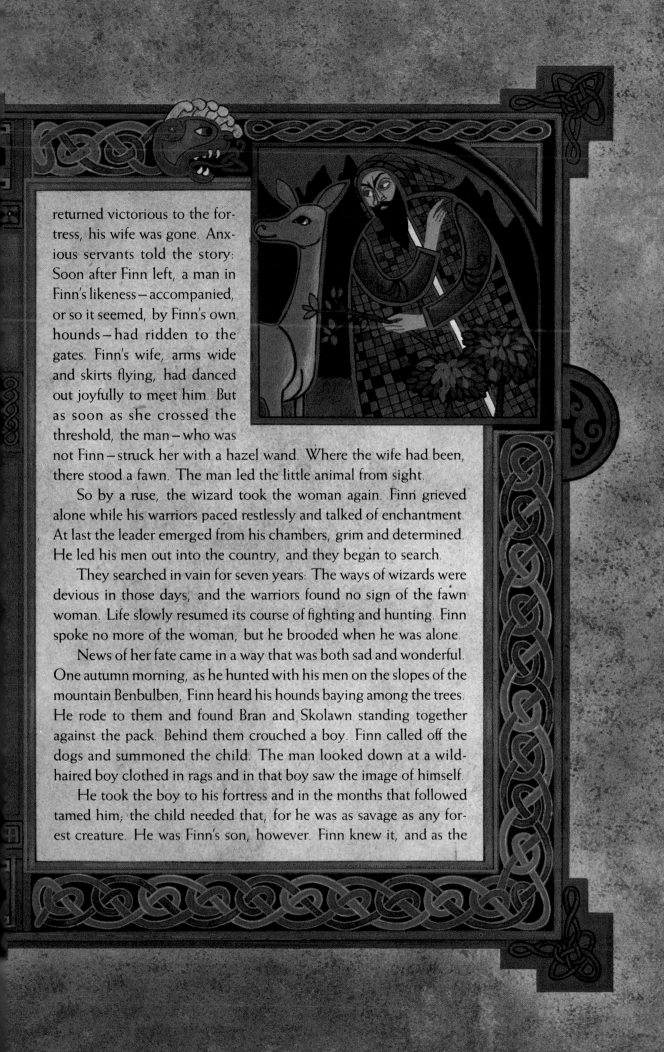

returned victorious to the fortress, his wife was gone. Anxious servants told the story: Soon after Finn left, a man in Finn's likeness—accompanied, or so it seemed, by Finn's own hounds—had ridden to the gates. Finn's wife, arms wide and skirts flying, had danced out joyfully to meet him. But as soon as she crossed the threshold, the man—who was not Finn—struck her with a hazel wand. Where the wife had been, there stood a fawn. The man led the little animal from sight.

So by a ruse, the wizard took the woman again. Finn grieved alone while his warriors paced restlessly and talked of enchantment. At last the leader emerged from his chambers, grim and determined. He led his men out into the country, and they began to search.

They searched in vain for seven years: The ways of wizards were devious in those days, and the warriors found no sign of the fawn woman. Life slowly resumed its course of fighting and hunting. Finn spoke no more of the woman, but he brooded when he was alone.

News of her fate came in a way that was both sad and wonderful. One autumn morning, as he hunted with his men on the slopes of the mountain Benbulben, Finn heard his hounds baying among the trees. He rode to them and found Bran and Skolawn standing together against the pack. Behind them crouched a boy. Finn called off the dogs and summoned the child. The man looked down at a wild-haired boy clothed in rags and in that boy saw the image of himself.

He took the boy to his fortress and in the months that followed tamed him; the child needed that, for he was as savage as any forest creature. He was Finn's son, however. Finn knew it, and as the

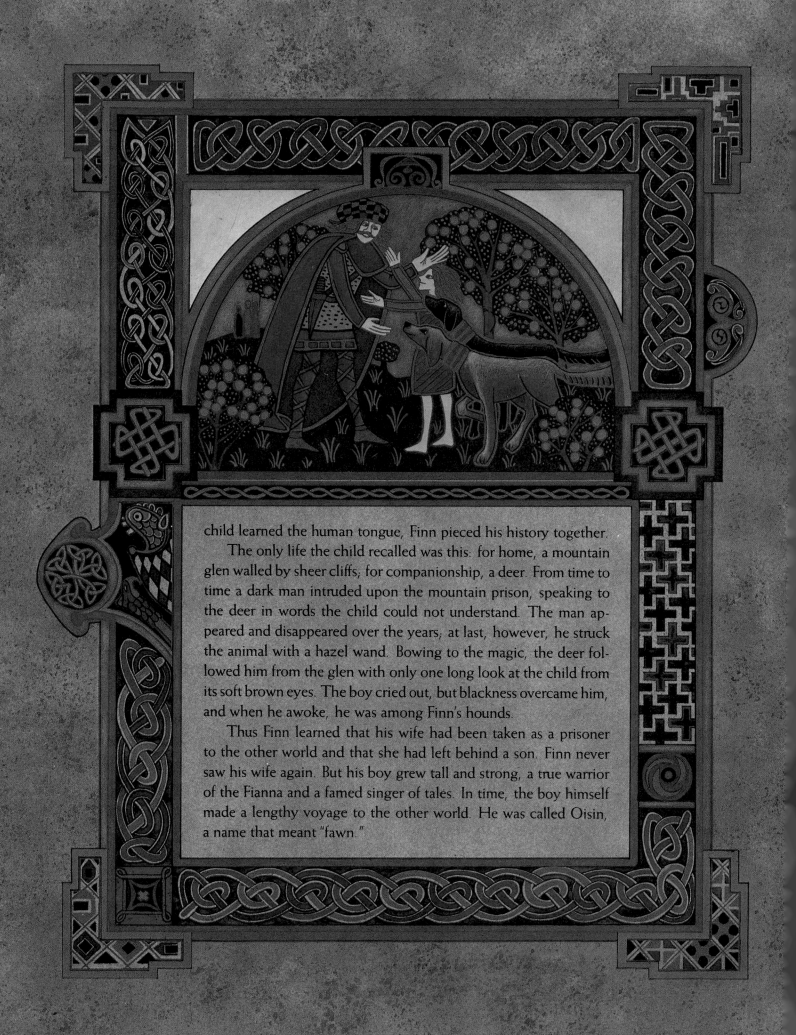

child learned the human tongue, Finn pieced his history together.

The only life the child recalled was this: for home, a mountain glen walled by sheer cliffs; for companionship, a deer. From time to time a dark man intruded upon the mountain prison, speaking to the deer in words the child could not understand. The man appeared and disappeared over the years; at last, however, he struck the animal with a hazel wand. Bowing to the magic, the deer followed him from the glen with only one long look at the child from its soft brown eyes. The boy cried out, but blackness overcame him, and when he awoke, he was among Finn's hounds.

Thus Finn learned that his wife had been taken as a prisoner to the other world and that she had left behind a son. Finn never saw his wife again. But his boy grew tall and strong, a true warrior of the Fianna and a famed singer of tales. In time, the boy himself made a lengthy voyage to the other world. He was called Oisin, a name that meant "fawn."

curfew and shut his house against the dangers of the night. From within the sheltering walls drifted the sound of singing: The company was feasting in the hall. But the boy was left out, alone in the fading light.

He saw a movement by the gate. An immense mastiff — a dog bred for its guardian's role — rose slowly from the ground. Its eyes glittered, the hair stood up on its back, and from deep in its throat, a low growl began. The animal had been unchained for the night. Setanta stopped at once, clutching his hurling ball, for he had no wish to be savaged by a dog. But the animal charged him.

It streaked across the grass toward the boy, howling like a hound of hell. He had a flashing image of bared and gleaming fangs; he smelled the rank breath, and Setanta acted. He thrust the hurling ball deep into the animal's hot throat. The creature checked and gagged, unable to bite because of the golden ball, and Setanta wrenched back his hand. He grasped the mastiff's legs and threw the beast down. Then he smashed its huge head against a rock, again and again, until the the twitching of the body stopped.

Gasping for breath, Setanta rose to his feet — to face a row of tall men who, drawn by the noise, had opened the gate of the stockade. Looking down at Setanta were his uncle Conchobar, pale-faced with anxiety; Conchobar's warriors, wiping their mouths; and the smith himself, dark and tight-lipped.

"Boy," said the smith slowly, "there is no welcome for you here. You have killed my hound that ranged my land and guarded my house. No other hound can match it, and without that beast, all I have is at risk." And he turned his back on the child.

But the boy's response showed his noble spirit. He told the smith that if there was another whelp of the breed to be had, he would train it. And until the pup was large enough to serve, Setanta said, he himself would guard the land of the smith.

"A fair offer," commented the King.

And although — being a royal child — Setanta was not allowed to serve as watchdog, he got his name from the offer. The King's sorcerer and wise man, Cathbad, gave it, to mark the spirit the child had shown. The name was Cuchulain, or in their language "the Hound of Culann."

It was a word of Cathbad's that prompted Cuchulain some time later to ask for the arms of an adult warrior. Cathbad had a part in the boys' training, and one day while he had charge of them, he was asked, as was the custom, what the day was good for; that is to say, what it portended.

The sorcerer replied that whoever received his arms that day would have the greatest name in Ireland, but his life would be a short one.

Open-hearted, longing for a hero's fame, the young Cuchulain seized his chance; as he himself said, it mattered nothing to him if his life lasted one day and one night only, so long as his name lived after him. He demanded his arms from the King his uncle. Those he received were Conchobar's own spears and sword and shield, for all the others offered were too flimsy for Cuchulain's strong hands. And the King gave the youth his own chariot and a charioteer named Loeg, who was to stay with him to the very end of Cuchulain's last battle.

His boyhood was over. Cuchulain set about the business of proving himself a man. Trained as he was in weaponry and battle, and schooled by the bravest and most learned of Conchobar's court, he had still to be blooded. He found his first combat in short order, by venturing across the Ulster border to challenge three brothers who periodically raided the province. He returned to Emain Macha, still in his battle fury, the dripping heads of his opponents dangling from the chariot rails and bouncing against the bars.

The trophies were the mark of triumph: Celtic warriors—believing in the soul and in the power that resides in the head—collected the skulls of the vanquished. Celtic temples and houses had niches that held the grinning bone faces of enemies, whose spirits served as protection for those who prayed or dwelled within.

"They cut off the heads of enemies slain in battle and attach them to the necks of their horses," wrote the Roman historian Diodorus Siculus of the Celtic tribes. "They embalm in cedar oil the heads of the most distinguished enemies and preserve them carefully in a chest and display them with pride to strangers."

**C**uchulain's fame mounted with the number of his trophies; he was called the bravest of Ireland's warriors and the first in beauty. Yet still his training was not finished.

The thread of his fate spun out in the way of heroes. As others before and after him, he ventured to the other world called Alba (*page 35*), where from the woman warrior Scathach he learned the magical arts that only the greatest knew: It was said that after Alba he could produce a thunderclap from his throat, dance on the head of a spear, slice an enemy through with the rim of his shield. He learned the use of the *gae bolga* – the vicious bone spear used only in extremity, whose saw-toothed head was shaped to shred an enemy's flesh as it was withdrawn after a thrust. In Alba, too, he fathered a son, who was to prove his sorrow. When he returned to Ireland again, he won its most beautiful maiden, Emer the Fair, for his wife and became, as has been shown, the champion of the King.

And all of this was still preliminary, preparation for the battle that poets would sing of for a thousand years. It began soon after Cuchulain became the King's champion, and its circumstances were these:

Peace was always uncertain among the five Irish kingdoms: Ulster in the north, Connacht in the west, Leinster in the east, and the two Munsters—east and west—at the southern tip of the island. Ulster was the strongest of the five, with Conchobar its King and Cuchulain its champion, but Ulster had enemies everywhere.

Chief among these enemies was Maeve, the Queen of Connacht, ruling from her bronze-pillared palace in a fortress on the hill of Cruachan. Pale-haired Maeve was Queen in her own right, for the crown of Connacht passed through the female line; she was a valiant warrior and, some said, a sorceress. She ruled her husband Ailill

*Magnificent but malevolent was Maeve of Connacht, a warrior Queen who sent*
*vast armies to conquer the champions of Ulster and seize the magic bull of Cooley.*

with a hand of iron. She kept her lovers in the palace itself, and Ailill was never heard to complain.

One morning, however, as the couple lay late in bed, Ailill crossed his wife.

"Good is the wife of a good man," he observed sententiously.

"True," replied Maeve. "And what brings that to mind?"

"You are a better woman now than when I married you," Ailill said.

There was a short and furious silence.

"I was good before I ever had to do with you," snapped Maeve.

And so began the famous pillow talk that led to the death of thousands of Ireland's greatest warriors. Maeve and Ailill, comparing their virtues, soon came to quarrel over whose possessions were richer. They totted up their separate properties—their jewels and silks, their flocks and herds, even their pots, tubs, buckets and jugs, and the score was even.

But Ailill had something that Maeve lacked—a mighty white bull called Finnbennach. The bull's power and ferocity were unmatched in Ireland, with only one exception. At Cooley in Ulster dwelled the Donn, a great brown bull said to be able to sire fifty calves in a day. Maeve determined to have the Donn of Cooley for her own and so best her husband.

The tale began thus trivially, but the two bulls were no mere herd animals. Maeve was tampering with things she should have left alone. The animals were bull lords, protectors of the people and of the fertility of the herds. They once had had human form, it was said. The white bull had been a servant of the Side—the fairy princes—of Connacht, the brown bull of the Side of Munster. When they were in that form, a rivalry developed between them and in their raging, the two began to shift in shape.

The pair were seen as ravens, prophesying war; the two were seen later as water beasts, devouring each other. At last, in the form of water serpents, they were swallowed by cows, which subsequently gave birth to the two finest bulls in Ireland—Finnbennach and the Donn of Cooley. When those enchanted animals were safe apart in separate provinces, the country flourished. What Maeve was planning, however, would wreak havoc: When the bull lords fought, death stalked the land. But in her pride and greed, Maeve cared nothing for the danger. She decided to steal the Donn of Cooley.

She summoned a host of warriors and found eager allies. The plain surrounding Cruachan soon flickered with a thousand campfires. Maeve's seven sons came with their troops, the King of Leinster with his and the Munster Kings with theirs. And among that host was Fergus, foster father of Cuchulain, and Cormac, Conchobar's son: These two had years before left Ulster to serve Maeve because Conchobar had done a dishonorable thing (page 56); they loved their own land still but they fought against it. And also there was Ferdiad, a brilliant warrior of Connacht who had trained with Cuchulain in Alba. Although the two were from different provinces, they were foster brothers because of what they had shared in the other world.

Maeve consulted a woman of the Side about the fate of her troops, and the woman said she saw the men covered with crimson blood. Maeve paid little heed to this. She knew that the men of Ulster lay under a curse: Generations before, a fairy woman of Ulster, then in her last month of pregnancy, had been forced by drunken mortal warriors to race on foot against a team of horses. The race had ended at the hill where Conchobar's fortress later stood. The woman had won it, and there on the hill, before the eyes of the jeering warriors, she had given birth to twins. The woman's name was Macha and the birth gave the hill its name: Emain Macha in Gaelic meant "Macha's Twins." In her final shame and agony the fairy had laid a fate on the men of Ulster. For nine generations, at certain times of great danger, the men should be prostrated with the weakness of childbirth, so that they could not defend themselves; until the weakness passed, Ulster was vulnerable to invasion.

And even now, in the fortress of Emain Macha, Conchobar and his warriors lay unable to fight or even to walk. Maeve had spies who told her this; she therefore marched her armies northeast from Connacht toward the Ulster border.

**B**ut some factors Maeve had not reckoned on. One was the Ulsterman Fergus' love of his homeland. He led the armies of Maeve, it is true; it was said that he was her lover. But he also sent warning ahead to his foster son Cuchulain. And there was Cuchulain himself. His father was no Ulsterman but

Lugh the sun god, and the fairy woman's curse therefore passed Cuchulain by. He was alone save for his charioteer, Loeg, who had been born in another kingdom; but he was also in the flower of his youth and vigor.

So Maeve's armies drove north and east until they came to the place called Ardcullin, at the very border of Ulster. They found a pillar stone there, marking the boundary. Around it was twisted an oak sapling, and on the sapling was cut Cuchulain's name and a message to Fergus and the other Ulstermen with Maeve: If they crossed the border that night, it said, then they would die at sunrise.

They saw no other sign of Cuchulain, but they camped at the border that night. Snow fell with the darkness, but the next day dawned bright and cold; the sun shone on the snow, and heartened, the armies of Maeve pushed on into Ulster, sending two young warriors with their charioteers ahead as scouts.

Not many hours passed before they saw an oak tree standing black in the snow ahead. It had been stripped of all its branches but four, and each of these branches pierced the shredded neck of a blood-clotted head. The heads belonged to Maeve's two scouts and their chariot drivers. The killer was nowhere to be seen, but it was clear that Ulster's defense had begun. Fergus warned Maeve of what was coming. She pressed on: The troops were anxious, and she knew that Conchobar and his warriors lay prostrate at Emain Macha. She ignored the deadly presence of Cuchulain, the Hound of Ulster.

The harrying began. An army on the

move—with its chariots, horses, supply wagons and cattle—was a cumbersome and unwieldy thing. This was true especially when that army marched on unfamiliar, forest-crowded, river-laced ground, hampered by the snows and winds and fogs of winter. The days were exhausting in this strange and hostile land. And the nights were filled with terror for Maeve's men. In the darkness, the invaders heard the thundering of horses' hoofs, the creak of chariot wheels, the slapping of harnesses. Before they could group and turn for the battle, Cuchulain was upon them. Scouts and outriders died; outlying detachments were slaughtered to a man. At daybreak all along the track ahead, Maeve's warriors would find the dripping heads of their comrades, spiked to the branches of the trees.

Nights came when Cuchulain rode screaming into the full light of the campfires, his legs braced in the chariot behind his tall shield, his spears bristling in his hand. Beside him, hands like iron on the reins, eyes narrowed in perfect concentration, Loeg guided the horses in unerring circles that cut victims from the crowd to face Cuchulain.

The champion's battle fury was upon him; a golden glow, the hero light, could be seen playing about his head. Cuchulain was one against many, but the war goddess was in him then and Maeve's invaders died in their hundreds. It was said that some perished of fright because in his raging, a terrible transformation came upon Cuchulain. His hair, the soldiers whispered, stood on end, and from his scalp rose a fountain of black blood. It was said that one of his eyes closed and withdrew until it was almost invisible, while the other opened until he was one-eyed, like the Norse war god, Odin. His mouth gaped wide to reveal ferocious teeth. His body shook like a tree in the flood.

Hundreds upon hundreds of Maeve's army died. And death came close to Maeve

herself, where she stood in her own chariot, flanked by her generals. With derisive accuracy, during one attack, an iron ball from Cuchulain's sling killed the golden bird that sat upon the Queen's shoulder.

She halted the snail-like advance of her troops after four nights of slaughter and sent heralds to treat with Cuchulain. The heralds would be safe: Cuchulain did not slaughter messengers or any other unarmed men. They found him encamped with Loeg at a ford that crossed the Dee River where it neared the sea on Ulster's east coast. Cuchulain laughed at Maeve's message: She offered him great rewards to desert his own people and join her ranks. He did say, however, that he would bargain personally with her or with Fergus. So at last, with his foster father Fergus, Cuchulain struck an agreement: Each day the Ulster hero would take his stand at the ford. Each day Maeve would send one of her own champions to challenge him in single combat. While the fight went on, Maeve's army could march into Ulster; as soon as Cuchulain defeated the champion, however, the army had to halt and camp for that day.

It was not an unusual arrangement. Celtic armies habitually met in all their strength and masses, shaking their weapons, screaming taunts and boasts and blowing in harsh and deafening chorus the dragon-headed trumpets known as carynxes. At a signal the clamor ceased and the battle was joined by the opposing armies' champions, who decided the issue by single combat. That was the way in the age of heroes. Single combat gave glory where glory was due, and it spared lives in an age when every life was needed. Or, as Maeve remarked when she agreed to the terms, "It is better to lose one man every day than a hundred every night."

So day after day Maeve sent her champions against Cuchulain. And day after day they died. While they fought, Maeve sent a detachment racing north to Cooley and took the Donn; the bull was brought into her own camp. But not one man could get past Cuchulain at the ford.

It was whispered that his strength was such that the Morrigu—the death-lustful war goddess—came to him in the night, scarlet-haired and robed in scarlet. She offered herself to him, but Cuchulain refused her, having other things to do. Raging, she tried to hamper him in battle. She took the form of an eel in the ford and twisted around his legs as he fought; he slashed at the creature and blinded it.

It was said that, desperate at last, Maeve sent six warriors, all of them enchanters, instead of one, and that Cuchulain killed them all. Then, in his rage at her betrayal, he came in the night and savaged Maeve's army, as he had done before. It was said that then, when Cuchulain began to falter from the weeks of fighting and his wounds, the sun god, Lugh, appeared beside him and sent him to sleep for three days, that he might rest and heal, while Lugh himself took Cuchulain's shape and fought in his place.

And there were Fergus, Cuchulain's foster father, and Ferdiad, his brother-in-arms, both fighting for Maeve when it was Cuchulain they loved in their hearts.

*To stop Cuchulain's harrying of her armies, Maeve and her general, Fergus, made this bargain: If Cuchulain would fight her champions one by one, her armies would not move as long as he remained the victor.*

Maeve sent Fergus first. Fergus went to the ford in the morning and halted his chariot on the south side. While his horses stamped and whinnied, Fergus called out to his foster son.

"For the sake of all I did for you in your youth, give way before me on this day," cried Fergus.

Cuchulain refused.

Then Fergus said, "But here is my word. If you give way today, I will give way when you need me most. In the last battle, I will turn and run before you, and the armies of Maeve will run with me." And though he was loath to do it, Cuchulain fell back before his foster father. That day Maeve's armies tore deep into Ulster, looting and burning as they went.

Ferdiad was a different matter. That young man—the brightest of Maeve's warriors, trained with Cuchulain in the mists of Alba—refused steadfastly to fight the companion of his boyhood. He refused when Maeve offered honors and plunder. He refused when she offered her daughter for his wife. But Maeve was cunning. She swore that she would make the bards of every Irish province sing of Ferdiad's cowardice against Cuchulain. After that, Ferdiad did not refuse: He could not bear the thought of such a stain on his honor.

At dawn of the day, therefore, Ferdiad armed himself and drove to the ford and waited on the south bank. The light had not struck the water before he saw Cuchulain coming through the trees, with Loeg, the charioteer, beside him. Cuchulain's golden hair shone as it had in his child-hood; his eyes were shadowed with his tiredness, but he smiled upon his old companion Ferdiad.

"In our youth," said Cuchulain, "we fought together because we were matched in skill and in valor. You were my people then, you were my family. No one is dearer. Do not fight me now." He told Ferdiad of Maeve's trickeries. He said that heart's companions should not fight.

But Ferdiad said merely, "Why delay? What arms shall we use, then?" Ferdiad's driver turned his head away.

After a moment, Cuchulain smiled again. He replied, "Yours is the choice of arms, for you were first at the ford."

Ferdiad chose casting spears, light weapons with which they had practiced long hours when they were boys. So each took his shield and the ivory-hafted short spears, eight for each. From the dancing chariots they fought, casting the spears over the waters quickly, and as quickly they feinted and dodged while the chariot drivers sweated at the reins. All the morning they rallied, and so evenly were they matched that neither was wounded.

When the sun rose high, Ferdiad said, "Light spears are not the weapons that will settle this." Cuchulain agreed, and they changed to heavier straight spears, those that were retrieved after the cast with flaxen lines. They fought through the afternoon, and both were wounded.

Yet when the shadows lengthened, Ferdiad and Cuchulain at once threw the spears to their drivers and held out their hands. That night they stabled the horses together in one enclosure made of branches; the drivers shared one fire; and

the two young warriors shared their food and talked in the way that old friends talk.

The next day it was the same and the day after that; they fought steadily with the broad spear and then with the sword. They wounded each other and the blood trickled into their eyes. They lurched with exhaustion and still they fought on.

At the end of the third day, however, the two drew apart to their separate banks of the ford. They bade each other farewell then, and each on his bed of rushes stared alone at the silent stars.

Morning came clear and bright and full of singing birds. Ferdiad armed himself in his breastplate of iron. His helmet was studded with carbuncle and crystal. His curved sword at his side and his shield slung across his back, he gazed across the water at his friend and enemy Cuchulain.

The Ulster champion gazed back. Then he turned and said to Loeg the driver, "We fight on foot today. If I should falter, jeer at me to give me the strength of anger." Loeg nodded and stepped back.

Then the warriors swung their shields across their bodies and stepped into the shallow waters of the ford. All morning long they cast until at length they fought shield to shield, struggling together on the slippery rocks.

Cuchulain broke the deadlock; he leaped at Ferdiad, who threw him down once, and then again.

"Coward Cuchulain," hissed faithful Loeg from the riverbank. "Little weakling, what claim to honor have you?"

Cuchulain listened to the ugly words for a moment. He rose to his knees in the

## An evil ruse that came to naught

Day after day during the battle for the Donn of Cooley, Cuchulain, the champion of Ulster, slaughtered Connacht's champions in single combat at the ford on the River Dee. But at last the Connacht Queen played a dastardly trick: She sent the warrior Calatin to fight the Ulsterman, but Calatin was not alone. His twenty-eight sons came with him. Some say that all twenty-nine men were one – a horribly joined monster warrior with twenty-nine heads – but this merely meant that they were of one blood and so marvelously skilled that they fought as one.

From dawn to dusk Cuchulain fought that vicious tribe with spear and sword and battle-ax. He might easily have fallen, for the odds against him were great. But when the press was at its worst, a traitor gave him aid: An Ulsterman fighting for Connacht – yet still tied by old loyalties – leaped into the fray. Thus heartened, Cuchulain killed; he took the heads of Calatin and of all Calatin's sons.

The battle was won for that day. But Calatin had a wife who was with child, and the creatures that she bore were brought up to be instruments of vengeance against the man who had slain their father.

water and then swayed to his feet. Light began to play around his head. In the distance both men heard a wild chorus, as if in sympathy the ravens of Ulster were calling for the kill.

The warriors' swords were in their hands: Ferdiad struck around Cuchulain's shield so that the blade opened the champion's side and the water played red around his feet. A mad light gleamed in Cuchulain's eyes then. He thrust his hand out and shouted hoarsely, and Loeg, waiting on the riverbank, sent flying the *gae bolga*, the vicious barbed spear that could gut a man.

Ferdiad, hearing the shout, turned at once to the side and swung his shield up to guard his belly. He moved too late. The *gae bolga* leaped from Cuchulain's hand past the rim of the shield into Ferdiad's breastplate, and tore through his body. The barbed point appeared behind his back, piercing the air where he stood.

"I die by that," cried Ferdiad. "I die by that, and it is on your head, Cuchulain." Bright blood bubbled from his mouth. His shield dropped, and he lurched forward.

*C*uchulain's arms were there to catch him; it was Cuchulain who lifted Ferdiad and carried him to the north bank of the ford, so that Ferdiad might die in Ulster and not among the armies of Maeve.

He sang the lament for Ferdiad to give his friend honor equal to his own. All fights, Cuchulain sang, were games and jests save for those he had fought with Ferdiad, the friend of his youth. Ferdiad had been a mountain, he sang, and now he was less than a shadow. All fury spent, Cuchulain rested on the bank beside the body. Loeg anxiously summoned him away, but Cuchulain did not hear.

A curious thing happened then. Creeping from the trees and underbrush came men of Ulster to bear the champion Cuchulain away. The curse was passing from them. It always did, in time. They had now to rally, for with Cuchulain down, Maeve's armies began a long sweep into Ulster, burning the villages and firing the fields. They killed as they went.

It was said that in the weeks that followed, Cuchulain was hidden in the care of the Side. They knew the ways of leaves and herbs and how to ease the spirit. In those weeks, Conchobar the King rallied his men to him. To Emain Macha they came, and when they had massed they set out after Maeve.

The battle raged across the countryside for days, until the trees were bare and blackened and the fresh fields no more than charred stubble. But Maeve's armies, having taken their plunder — and won the Donn of Cooley — at last prepared to withdraw. Conchobar followed, harrying and killing until Fergus brought his armies around again, to drive back the Ulster King.

And this was the last battle where Cuchulain appeared on the field. Above the din, Fergus heard Cuchulain's voice.

"Go back now, Fergus," he shouted. Fergus refused.

"You are bound by your oath, Fergus," Cuchulain cried. "The oath you gave at the ford, when I fell back for you."

*Of all Cuchulain's duels the cruelest for him was the one he was forced to fight with Ferdiad, the companion of his boyhood. Ferdiad fell. He died in his friend's arms, and Cuchulain sang the lament for him.*

That was true. Fergus stepped back. He turned his chariot and gave way for Cuchulain. His men turned with him, and Maeve's army, seeing this, broke ranks and fled. The men of Ulster followed after, killing, until little was left of the Connacht invaders but the dead and the dying.

In the field then, Cuchulain came upon Maeve. She was almost alone. Her proud chariot was shattered; her golden hair was crusted with blood and her face blackened with dirt. On her knees, she begged the champion for safe conduct. He gave it, and that was a mistake. Maeve and Ailill and the remnants of the great army made the long march to Cruachan, their hearts filled with rage at the shame Cuchulain had brought upon them.

As for the cause of the war, Maeve took it with her on the retreat, but she had no pleasure from it. She had eight messengers lead the Donn of Cooley to Connacht. This they managed to do. When they brought the bull to Cruachan, however, it got scent of the White Bull of Connacht and there was no holding it. The great animals pawed the earth and shook the ground and broke loose from their chains and charged. All who were near enough to see the battle died, for the bulls trampled them to red pulp upon the ground.

The last that was seen of the Brown Bull in Maeve's country was his great horns flecked with the flesh of the White Bull of Connacht. The bull lord headed northeast to Ulster. And when the bull arrived in Cooley a madness came upon it; it killed the people it could find and trampled the fields. Then it sank to the ground and died. In its rage, its heart had burst.

Thus ended the war for the Great Brown Bull of Cooley, with death and destruction, starvation and pain. Maeve had slunk back to Connacht, defeated—in the main—by one man's arms. Beaten and shamed, she stayed there.

But Maeve and those with her had vengeance in their hearts. And the man they would seek was the author of defeat—Cuchulain, the champion of Ulster.

# A Champion's Schooling in Another World

Heroes ventured where the mass of humankind dared not tread—into the shifting shadow worlds that once lay hidden within the solid landscapes of everyday. The voyages were perilous, but the rewards were great: On one such journey, the Irish warrior Cuchulain passed from youth to manhood.

His adventure began as a test: Cuchulain desired a woman called Emer the Fair, whose father demanded that he prove himself at the school of the legendary woman warrior Scathach. She ruled Alba, a land far beyond the mist and spindrift of the restless Irish Sea.

With three companions, Cuchulain sailed to Alba's rocky shore. In days, the companions vanished, seduced away, it was said, by magic. The young Ulster warrior traveled on alone, heading north until he came to a plain that stretched to the rim of the sky, where bony mountain ranges loomed. Steaming and shivering, the plain was bad land; it seethed with spells. Cuchulain hesitated, and when he did, a child appeared to him, offering talismans. If he wished to find Scathach, said the strange child gravely, he must follow the talismans.

Cuchulain took them. The first was a wheel, which he cast on the plain. At once the wheel glowed gold and of its own rolled off. As the child had advised,

Cuchulain followed, although on either side pitch welled up, black, boiling and deep enough to trap a man forever.

In the wheel's track he was safe. When the golden disk vanished, Cuchulain threw the second talisman—a golden apple—and followed as it rolled ahead. On either side, swaying like grain in the wind, grew glittering knives, sharp enough to sever a man's legs. In the apple's track, however, Cuchulain was untouched and thus passed in safety the outer barriers to Scathach's world.

He left the plain at last and trudged on, ascending steadily into darkening mountains, until at dusk he saw the fortress of the woman warrior. Perched on a cold promontory, the stronghold was embraced by a windy chasm. The pit was arched by a narrow bridge. Encamped on the ledge in front of the bridge were the youths who would become the Ulsterman's companions in training, the warrior band of Scathach. They were a fine crew, bright-haired and strong-limbed. They jeered at him, an unproven stranger. One shouted to Cuchulain that he should try the bridge, and that was a trick, for the bridge of its own power could cast the foolhardy into the chasm below.

Cuchulain leaped onto the span. Like a wave beneath him, the bridge swayed and buckled; he felt it snap upward and landed, gasping, back on the ledge. The youths jeered the louder. He tried again and once again, and each time, the bridge tossed him to the ledge amid a chorus of derision.

Cuchulain brightened with rage then, and the hero light blazed around his head, so that his tormentors fell silent. They saw him leap once more into the air, touch the bridge and spring across the span as a salmon leaps upstream. With a spear, he struck the for-

tress gates. Behind him, the bridge swayed supple as silk in the wind.

It was the last barrier. The massive fortress gates swung open. Knowing Cuchulain's worth, Scathach received him: Only the valiant could breach her barriers, and around this man's head shone the glowing light of the hero.

Thus she took Cuchulain into her company and trained him. He spent long months in Alba, learning battle skills charged with magic, skills so strange that while their names were long remembered, later generations, having lost the arts, could not tell exactly what the skills might be. Some of their names were: the blade feat, the spear feat, the rope feat, the salmon feat and the whirl of the brave chariot chief.

Cuchulain learned well, so well that no one lacking other-world training—and few in Alba itself—would be a match for him. He led Scathach's band. He fought for her in her own battles and thereby got his only son:

As Cuchulain's training neared its end, a rival of Scathach's thundered through the mountain passes at the head of an invading army. The challenger was called Aifa, and she was a warrior queen of great prowess. Scathach's cadre of heroes met the invaders, but it was Cuchulain alone who slew Aifa's champions. Then, as was the custom, Aifa challenged Scathach to single combat.

But Cuchulain demanded to stand for his mentor. Although he was warned of Aifa's ferocity, all he asked was to know what she cherished. Scathach told him: Aifa loved her horses, chariot and charioteer. Then Cuchulain went forth to battle.

They fought with spears, but the spears shattered harmlessly. The two were closely matched in spear play. When they turned to swords, however,

the woman swiftly disarmed the man, her blade flashing up in the dusty air and breaking Cuchulain's from its hilt.

But the Ulsterman was crafty. He shouted that Aifa's chariot and horses had stumbled at the cliff edge and were in danger of sliding over. Caught by the trick, Aifa turned her gaze for one instant, and in that instant, Cuchulain seized her in his arms.

His grip was like iron; he threw Aifa to the ground and pressed his dagger to her throat, demanding surrender. And she yielded to him. She promised that she would fight Scathach no more. She said that she would give herself to Cuchulain, who had conquered her. Thus Cuchulain took Aifa to her camp and kept her by him for some weeks. He got her with child in that time and told her what he knew in his heart. The child, Cuchulain said, would be a son.

"Send the boy to me in Ulster when he is seven," said Cuchulain. Without another word, he left Aifa, never seeing the light of vengeance that gleamed behind her eyes.

Cuchulain's appointed year in Alba had drawn to its close, and so he returned to Scathach's fortress to make his farewell. The chieftainess then gave him who was the pride of her pupils the greatest of spears, the *gae bolga*. She blessed his valor. And she made this prophecy: that Cuchulain would triumph, one man over multitudes; that his greatness would live forever in the poets' songs; that his life would pass as quickly as the dew.

Cuchulain cared everything for the fame and nothing for the brevity of the warrior's life. He returned to Ulster, to the bride he had won and the glory that was to come. But he never spared a thought for his child, left behind in the shadow world of Alba.

# Chapter Two

# The Cruel Demands of Honor

At Samain, the Celtic feast day between summer and winter when the wind blew from the north and the sun's path sank low in the sky, the hero Cuchulain died at the hands of his enemies. The great Hound of Ulster died on his feet, having lashed himself to a pillar stone when he knew he had received the death blow. And mortally wounded though he was, none of his adversaries dared approach until the glowing radiance, called the hero light, faded from the air around him and a raven settled heavily on his shoulder. Then the enemies cut off Cuchulain's head and his right hand, and carried the trophies from Ulster.

He died in his prime, in the manner of heroes, and as it was for all of them, it was for him. They were men, it is true, but greater than men. They went to their inevitable ends not meekly but in glory, willingly embracing the common fate and making of that fate a triumph. For a hero, the pathway to death was strewn with portents. The moment he embarked upon this course, Cuchulain knew that each step would lead inexorably to the end. He accepted it and journeyed bravely.

The first portent was a young boy on a beach. This beach, a shingle washed by the gray-green waves of the Irish Sea on Ulster's east coast, was called Baile's Strand. Not far away stood Cuchulain's own fortress, Dundealgan, where it happened once that Conchobar, King of

Ulster, was holding court with Cuchulain and others of the Red Branch knights, the company of heroes who served the King.

On this day, word came to the fortress that a ship bearing armed warriors led by a bright-faced youth had beached at Baile's Strand, and Conchobar sent a messenger to learn the stranger's business. The messenger returned without an answer: The youth, he said, had refused to give his name or an account of himself. He had only laughed when the messenger warned him that if he did not tell it willingly, the information would be dragged from him.

When he heard that, Cuchulain called for his spears and sword and set off for Baile's Strand with the King and a company of Red Branch knights. There they found the boy leaning idly on his spear. Cuchulain paused to observe the stranger; he was a slender youth, but as finely muscled as a hunting hound, and he bore a champion's heavy spears and broadsword.

Cuchulain smiled and saluted the stranger courteously enough. "Now then, boy," he said easily. "Give over this folly and tell us your name."

But the boy shook his head. "I tell no man my name. I never refuse a battle, even though it mean my death," said he. Then he straightened and stepped back and brought up his shield to defend his side.

So battle was joined. Light-footed as great cats, the youth and the man thrust and feinted and dodged. Their spears glittered in the air only to rattle harmlessly against their shields and clatter onto the pebbles of the beach. Neither one, it seemed, had the advantage, and that was strange indeed, because it was said that no man alive was a match for Cuchulain in his prime.

But a stranger thing followed. While the Red Branch knights watched, the youth began to press the older man, backing him steadily toward the water. Step by step, thrust by thrust, the boy advanced and the man retreated, not fighting easily now, but fighting for his life.

Cuchulain grew angry then. His lips tightened and his eyes narrowed; he called for the *gae bolga*, the cruelly barbed spear used only in extremity. It was thrown to him, and as he grasped it, his battle fury came full upon him. All around his head, the radiant hero light began to shine.

When he saw this, the boy checked, frozen in the act of casting his own spear. Then he cast, but all those watching could see that he threw to miss. The weapon sailed harmlessly past Cuchulain and in that instant, the older warrior cast the *gae bolga*—but not to miss. It flew with deadly ease past the rim of the youth's shield and slid swift and deep into his belly. The battle was done; the spear's wound was always mortal. The shield fell from the boy's shoulder and he sank to the ground. Cuchulain strode forward to finish the kill.

But the boy raised his hand so that Cuchulain saw the golden ring he wore. "I am my mother's instrument," he said. But Cuchulain, kneeling over him, already knew the truth of the matter—the ring and the valor of the boy had told him.

The youth was his son. Long years before, when Cuchulain received his champion's training in the other world of Alba,

east across the sea, he had conquered a woman warrior and gotten her with child (*page 41*). He had left the woman to take his rightful place in Ulster, but he had given her a golden ring for the child that was to come, telling her that it would be a boy and that when the boy was of the age to bear arms she should send him to Ulster.

And she had done so. But his dying son told Cuchulain all that she had done. Enraged by Cuchulain's conquest and desertion, she had had the child trained in battle skills until there was nothing more to teach him; there was no youth in Alba as valiant as he. And then she made him into a weapon of revenge. She gave him the arms of a champion and sent him to Ulster to find his father. And she laid three magical bonds upon him, promises that upon his life and honor he could never break. The first was never to be turned aside by any living person; the second not to refuse a challenge from the greatest man alive; and the third, never to tell his name.

Thus the woman warrior ensured that the son would kill the father or the father the son. The boy lay now on the shingle, blood bubbling at his lips, and gasped out how he had turned his spear aside when he saw the hero light and recognized his father; he told of the bonds that had made it impossible for him to speak and at last he told his name: "I am Conla, son of the Hound of Ulster," he said, and the light began to fade from his eyes.

Then Cuchulain, kneeling beside him, wept. With his own sword, he struck the youth through the heart to spare him the agony of long dying. So Cuchulain killed his only son. He threw back his head then and gave a great howl of grief, as if his heart and not Conla's had been pierced by the sword. He sang and the song was carried out over the waves:

"I am the father that killed his son, the fine green branch; there is no hand or shelter to help me. I am a raven that has no home; I am a boat going from wave to wave; I am a ship that has lost its rudder; I am the apple left on the tree; it is little I thought of falling from it. Grief and sorrow will be on me from this time."

Madness came upon Cuchulain then and the Red Branch knights bore him to his fortress that he might rest and heal. But Cuchulain had not long to live, for his final battle was nearing. Many said his dying began that day on Baile's Strand, when all unknowing, he killed his only son.

The events that led to Cuchulain's last battle on the Plain of Muirthemne were already set in motion. In those days, honor required that what one suffered be repaid in kind. As it was for the woman Cuchulain conquered, so it was for the warriors of Ireland: Vengeance was all. And Cuchulain – the slaughterer of the Irish at the battle of Cooley – had enemies in plenty, waiting for revenge.

Chief among them was Maeve, the warrior Queen of Connacht, whose armies had been destroyed at the battle of Cooley. Maeve brooded and waited, and her time came at last, when those she had chosen as weapons had grown into their strength. The first she called were honed to sharpness by the warrior Queen herself. It had happened that during the battle,

Cuchulain had slain one of Maeve's champions, a warrior called Calatin, and his sons with him (*page 31*); shortly thereafter, Calatin's widow had given birth to triplets, twisted, one-eyed female creatures. Maeve recognized the trio for the demons they were and sent them to the dark corners of the world to learn the magic arts.

When they returned, skilled in the making of illusion, in the shifting of shape and in prophecy, Maeve summoned a council. Especially, she called Erc, son of the King of Leinster, whose bloodied head Cuchulain had brandished before the Leinster troops. And she called Lugaid, son of a Munster King whom Cuchulain had also slain. To these and to Calatin's daughters, Maeve put the same question:

"Who slew your father?"

Each by each, they answered with Cuchulain's name. Then the battle for Cuchulain's life began.

**M**aeve moved her forces – her armies of Connacht, Lugaid with his Munster detachments and Erc with the men of Leinster – north to the borders of Ulster. With her went Calatin's daughters, those frightful hags, now squalling among the baggage vans, now cackling in tree branches, now crowding Maeve's chariot and whispering spells. The armies harried the borders for days.

At King Conchobar's stronghold of Emain Macha, the old illness – sufferings caused by a curse (*page 25*) – came upon the Red Branch knights. Conchobar knew what this meant; his warriors could not fight until their weakness passed. Concho-

bar knew, too, that although Cuchulain was not affected by the curse, he was weakened by his grief. He could not stave off the enemies alone, as he had before. Conchobar had no doubt about Maeve's plan: She meant to separate the hero from the rest and cut him down – and if she succeeded, Ulster would be defenseless.

Conchobar therefore ordered Cuchulain secluded, first within the fortress at Emain Macha and then in a remote royal hall. He surrounded the warrior with women and bards, whose songs and spells he hoped would calm Cuchulain's battle fury. At Conchobar's urging, Cuchulain's mistress, Niamh, made Cuchulain promise that he would not fight unless she gave him leave. Even with a pledge of honor and Conchobar's protection, Cuchulain was an easy mark for Maeve – and Maeve had the services of Calatin's daughters.

Each time Conchobar hid the hero, those sorceress-hags followed with the lightness of the wind. They sat on the sunny lawns of Emain Macha and of the royal hall – three twisted shadows crawling on the green. From stalks of grass and oak leaves and mushrooms, they fashioned phantom armies, which clashed in battle before Cuchulain's eyes and seemed to rend the very fabric of the land. Although he knew it was illusion, Cuchulain trembled with rage and eagerness to fight. Only his pledge to Niamh held him back.

And that not long. Because one of the hags took the fair shape of Niamh, and in Niamh's voice, she called to Cuchulain that Ulster was burning and the land laid waste without a defender.

Queen Maeve and her sorceries took

## Inexorable workings of man's fate

All heroes were netted in the web of fate: No power, said the poets, could prevail against untiring destiny. Thus every step taken to avert the fate of the Greek hero Oedipus only wrapped him closer in its strands.

It was prophesied by oracles before his birth that Oedipus would murder his father and wed his own mother. When he was born, therefore, his father, Laius, King of Thebes, had the infant's feet pierced and ordered him left in the wilderness to die.

But the child did not die: A shepherd took him south to Corinth, where the King and Queen of that land reared him as their own, so that he loved them as his parents.

the trick. Cuchulain girded for battle.

Then, thick as the rains of autumn and the winter snows, the omens of his own death clouded Cuchulain's path. When he armed himself, the golden brooch that pinned his war cloak fell from his hands and pierced his foot. In the fields where they grazed, his horses were skittish; they would not come for harnessing when the charioteer Loeg shook their bridles at them. They came only at Cuchulain's call and from the dark eyes of the lead stallion – called the Gray of Macha – streamed bloody tears.

Still the horses were harnessed and hitched to the chariot, and Loeg and Cuchulain set off, moving swiftly under a lowering sky. They raced through the forests of Ulster toward the Plain of Muirthemne, where Maeve's armies were gathered. Behind them they heard a high wailing – the keening of the women of Ulster.

His mother's house lay on the way, and while Loeg held the nervous horses, Cuchulain stopped for her blessing. She offered him wine, but the chalice brimmed with blood instead. Seeing it, his mother begged him not to go on, but Cuchulain only smiled and left her.

The light faded and the pair galloped on. They passed a stream where a pale young woman washed bloody clothing and wept. A voice called out that she wept for Cuchulain. He answered only that before he died, other clothes than his would be bloodied, and he drove on.

The last and bitterest omen was this. A small fire appeared on the side of the path. Around it hovered three old crones, their faces hidden within black hoods. Their

hands shone with grease in the firelight; they had spitted a dog and this they were roasting. They hailed Cuchulain by name and invited him to join the feast.

Now, this was a hard thing, for Cuchulain, like most Irish kings and heroes, lay under several *geasa*, or prohibitions or bonds, just as Cuchulain's son had been placed under bonds by his mother. A *geis* was a serious matter, concerning otherworld powers, and the breaking of the bond led to the death of the person who broke it. One of Cuchulain's *geasa* was that he would never eat the flesh of a dog. Another was that he would never refuse an offered feast.

Caught between the conflicting demands, Cuchulain hesitated. The old women jeered. At that he dismounted and joined their feast. He ate hound's flesh, holding a leg bone in his left hand, and the strength went out of the hand. He wiped the hand on his left thigh, and the strength went out of the thigh. Then, limping slightly, he climbed into the chariot beside his grim-faced driver and headed for the battle, while the cackling of the hags rose into the air and twisted in the tree branches.

Fate was quiet while Oedipus grew. When he became a young warrior, however, he heard the prophecy: that he would murder his father and marry his mother. Horrified – for Oedipus had a loving nature – he fled Corinth, seeking to avert such evil. He went north to Thebes, and the web of destiny began to form.

At a place on his journey where three roads met, an old man insulted the youth; in arrogant rage Oedipus slew the man. That was Laius, King of Thebes. All unknowing, Oedipus had fulfilled the first part of the prophecy.

Thebes was besieged: Its King was dead; its countryside ravaged by the Sphinx, a creature with a lion's body, a woman's head and a riddle. To answer her riddle was to save the people. Oedipus challenged the Sphinx. She asked: "What walks on four legs in the morning, on two at midday and on three in the evening?"

"Man," replied Oedipus, the fated one nearing his fate. The Sphinx died then, and the country was rescued. Oedipus was made King of Thebes for his deed and given the old King's widow for a wife. And so in ignorance, he embraced the prophecy.

The truth was revealed to him years later, when plague struck his kingdom as punishment for his crime. Oedipus learned who he was then. Only the King could make the atonement that saved the country, and Oedipus made it. He put out his own eyes, and guided by two women who were his daughters and sisters both, he wandered through Greece, no longer the King, but only a man. When he knew it at last, he found the peace of death. And he achieved a hero's fame for facing what he could not change.

## A choice of death before dishonor

The valiant died but did not surrender; they faced the end but did not cry for help. So the poets said in France when they sang of Roland, the Emperor Charlemagne's champion and hammer against the Saracens.

Roland was revered but he had an enemy in France – his own stepfather, Ganelon. On Roland's suggestion – innocently made – Ganelon was sent to demand surrender of the Saracens. Ganelon did not see the embassy as an honor; he saw it as a threat to his life. He protested. Roland only laughed.

With hatred in his heart, therefore, Ganelon went to treat with the enemy. And treat he did: He told the Saracens that if they feigned surrender to Charlemagne, they would have victory in the end. They agreed to the treachery. He then informed the Emperor that the Saracens would yield.

Then Charlemagne withdrew his forces from Spain, leaving a rear guard of twenty thousand, under the command of Roland, to protect the mountain passes at Roncevalles. The Saracens attacked almost at once, with a force many times larger than Roland's small army.

Into the pass the enormous host swept, white robes flying and scimitars ablaze. From the heights Roland saw them. He could have summoned aid: He had a hunting horn whose call could be heard across the mountains in France. But he scorned this as cowardice. He sounded the horn only at the end of the battle, when his army lay dying, and that call was a cry for vengeance, not a plea for aid. Roland died with his face turned toward Spain, unflinching to the last.

Charlemagne and his armies answered the call; it was said that the sun delayed its setting until the Emperor destroyed the Saracens. That vengeance done, he did another, for by then the traitor's name was known. Ganelon's punishment was this: Soldiers tied his limbs to the harnesses of four war horses, which charged in the four directions of the compass, tearing Ganelon into quarters.

He found the Plain of Muirthemne crowded with the linked shields of the Irish and the air dusty with the lime they used to coat the leather. Straight in among them he charged, screaming like thunder and shaking his shining spears. Scores fell before him until the plain was reddened with crushed bodies.

**C**uchulain was a fearsome enemy, but Maeve had a plan. The hag daughters of Calatin had told her that Cuchulain's spears would kill three kings that day, and she was determined to have those spears. She therefore stationed the bards of her people around the field. They were men of power and commanded obedience.

The first summoned Cuchulain from the fray and demanded a spear. Cuchulain refused it.

"I will give you a bad name, if you refuse me this boon," cried the bard.

Cuchulain regarded him impassively from the height of the chariot, for a bard's curse on a warrior's honor was a shame indeed. Then he hurled the spear at the man with a force that sent the blade through his eye and the shaft through his head.

But Lugaid of Munster, he who sought vengeance for his father, retrieved the weapon and wiped away the blood and pieces of brain and bone and hurled it at Cuchulain's chariot. It struck the driver, Loeg. Calatin's daughters, hovering above the battlefield, gibbered and howled their triumph: Cuchulain had lost his first spear. It had killed the king of charioteers.

A second bard called out. Again Cuchulain's spear was demanded; and again Cuchulain refused it.

"I will put a bad name on the province of Ulster if you refuse me the spear," cried the bard, and as before, Cuchulain flung it and killed the man. And as before, a vengeful enemy—Erc of Leinster—retrieved and flung the spear. It killed Cuchulain's horse, the Gray of Macha. The Ulster champion had lost his second spear, the king of horses had been killed with it, and the daughters of Calatin screamed black triumph.

Yet once more a bard summoned the hero in the heat of battle and demanded a spear on pain of curses on Cuchulain's kin. And yet again Cuchulain killed the bard and the hags howled the louder. For Lugaid of Munster pulled the spear from the victim's head and, with unerring aim, sent it through Cuchulain where he stood in the chariot, so that Cuchulain's flesh was ripped open and his intestines spilled out.

He knew he had his death wound and he leaned a moment on the chariot's rail, while the Irish warriors backed away, murmuring fearfully among themselves to see him standing with such a wound, as if he were immortal. Then the Hound of Ulster pressed his guts back into his belly and bound it with his battle sash. Slowly he dismounted and slowly walked to a lake that bordered the field. He washed himself, and as he did, an otter—called by the Irish the "water dog"—crept up to drink the blood that stained the water. With a stone, Cuchulain killed the beast and thus his last heroic act, like the first of his youth, was the slaying of a dog. With the leather thong that held his breastplate, he strapped his body to a pillar stone. Then the king of warriors died, alone among his enemies, standing on his feet.

The day turned black. The ravens of the battle goddess rode the winds above the Plain of Muirthemne and the sounds of their harsh calling rent the air. In icy sheets, the rains lashed down as if the very skies wept for the death of Cuchulain. For heroes were the hearts of their kingdoms' strength, and untold power resided in their persons. So much were they revered, in fact, that in Ireland, dead champions often were buried standing upright in full battle dress with their blind faces turned toward the lands of the enemy, silent sentinels under the earth.

Early death was the hero's fate. All of them walked, as Cuchulain had, a narrow, twisty path hedged with mortal conflict. Their obligations and duties, inevitably put in opposition, made a tragic pattern for their lives. Ironclad and inescapable, one claim was set against another, so that the honorable were forced to choose between dishonors and pay a tragic price.

Cuchulain, for instance, had a duty to obey his king and to protect his province. Yet he had also the obligation to avoid shame and to be ready always to exercise his powers, regardless of the outcome. Cu-

## The violent creed of vengeance

Perhaps because they were stronger than ordinary men, heroes were fated to endure greater suffering: Life-and-death choices were their bitter lot. Such was the fate of Orestes of Mycenae, who could fulfill his duty to avenge the murder of his father, Agamemnon, only by slaying the murderer – who was Orestes' own mother, Clytemnestra.

The cycle of revenge began with the Trojan War, when King Agamemnon sacrificed his daughter to the gods to get fair wind for his ships. When the war was won and Agamemnon sailed home triumphant, Clytemnestra, fired with rage for her child, murdered him with an ax as he bathed.

Then Clytemnestra set out to rule Mycenae in Agamemnon's place, which she did successfully with the aid of her lover, the beautiful and corrupt Aegisthus. She knew that there was danger: Her son Orestes had been taken to safety in the mountains after the murder, and vengeance was a son's duty. But the years passed peacefully. Clytemnestra's power grew.

Orestes matured into a fine young warrior. He knew his destiny but, it was said, made no move until the god Apollo himself forced the decision. Clytemnestra must die, and at Orestes' hand, to satisfy the god.

At last, Orestes acted. He went to Mycenae. With a sword, he butchered his mother's lover. He showed her the body before he killed her, too. His father was avenged. But for Orestes, the matricide could not rest; his punishment was implacable pursuit by the Erinyes, avenging goddesses who haunted him with visions of ghouls and dreams of hell; Orestes became a stranger to sleep and earthly peace.

chulain knew his death would be a disaster for Ulster and he knew by the signs that his death was near. But he had to fight: Any conflict between a hero's obligations to his lord and to valor itself had to be resolved in favor of that which made him a hero.

And this pattern of inner conflict was openly expressed, in Ireland and Britain, in the magical bonds of *geasa* that confined the actions of the valiant. *Geasa* were meant to serve as protections and as indications of rank. Thus the King of Ulster was forbidden to attack alone a boar in its den, a prohibition obviously designed to safeguard the precious person of the King. Cuchulain was forbidden to refuse a feast, a rule of courteous behavior for those of royal blood. But many *geasa* were made to avert supernatural evils. The Ulster King could not bathe in Loch Foyle, in the northernmost part of Ulster, on May Day. (May Day, being the interstitial period between winter and summer, was a period outside mortal definition, since it was neither one thing nor another. On that day the powers of the other world were strong and mortals at most risk.) And Cuchulain,

the Hound of Ulster, was forbidden to eat the animal that bore his name. In those days names were charged with meaning, profoundly linked to the thing they named; to harm one's namesake was little different from harming oneself.

This heroic imperative could be exploited by crafty enemies, as Cuchulain's other-world mistress did when she bound his son Conla with the *geasa* that led to Conla's death. Maeve, too, used the trickery of conflict when she sent Calatin's daughters to provoke Cuchulain and force forbidden meat on him, and when she ordered her bards to threaten his honor and thereby cost him his spears.

The source of the hero's greatness, then, was also the source of his vulnerability. And it was so not only when rules of valor were in conflict: The hero's very nature – his more than mortal beauty, his loving and generous heart – too often placed him at odds with his duty.

This was especially true in matters of love. The wife or lover of the hero introduced a new focus for his loyalty; she could become a pivot that diverted his faithfulness from king and comrades. Principles, after all, were one thing: The bloom of a cheek, the glint of hair in sunlight, the curve of a breast beneath bleached linen were quite another. These were things that could melt the iron compass of honor, making straight lines yaw into arabesques of quandary and doubt.

And when the woman who possessed them also possessed a disregard for her own duties – or a love that overcame

them – disaster followed. It had happened at King Conchobar's court in Ulster, when Cuchulain was a young knight still, and it led to dishonor and death.

A day of portents came. Conchobar's bard and wizard, Cathbad, sensed that time was out of joint; he rose with the first light and watched the skies. The day dawned clear and blue. When the sun was fully up, however, a staining cloud slid darkly over the horizon, leading others of its kind. The wind screeched all the morning and at noon the ground began to tremble. Strange sounds filled the afternoon air – of screaming, of waves seething on stones, of women's moans.

Night fell at last, ominously silent. An infant girl was born to the wife of the King's harper. Cathbad went at once to the harper's house and gazed upon the child. It was she the storm had brought, he said. She would become a woman of unparalleled beauty, but ill fortune would follow in her footsteps: Heroes and kings would contend for her; she would blight Ulster with a pox of graves. "Name her Deirdre," Cathbad said. The name meant "troubler."

Such infants were killed in those days, but this was the harper's only child. Seeking to thwart fate, therefore, he took her into the mountains. Behind a green hill he built a little house for her, roofed with green sod and walled about with apple trees. A bard named Levarcham – a scholarly woman and a friend to the harper – stayed with Deirdre as her nurse.

For fourteen years the child lived with Levarcham in her mountain fastness, growing into a maiden as beautiful as a swan. She was schooled in the knowledge and graces of the bards themselves. But save for Levarcham, Deirdre never saw another living person.

Until one night a hunter stumbled upon her hiding place. He saw Deirdre; later he told King Conchobar about her and such were his praises that the King himself traveled to the mountains to look upon the girl. What the King saw filled him with desire; over Levarcham's protests he took the maiden to his high-walled fortress at Emain Macha, intending to make her his bride. Conchobar heard Levarcham's warnings, but his only answer was a shrug. He had a strong and reckless will.

Conchobar gave Deirdre a year and a day to learn the ways of a king's house and observed with pleasure how she blossomed. He decked her in treasures. From her long braids swung the hollow golden spheres that princesses wore then, and her white neck was embraced with a curved collar of gold. Her tunics were fine linen, pinned at the shoulder with brooches of scrolled bronze, and her cloaks were of the sheerest wool. She was a bright flower

*Betrothed to the King of Ulster, Deirdre of the Sorrows eloped to Scotland with the three sons of Usnech. Conchobar the King sent his own kinsman, Fergus Mac Roy, as an envoy to tempt her back into his power.*

among the pale maidens of the court, and the King—heedless of Cathbad's warnings—watched her with lustful interest and waited for the year to pass.

But Deirdre hardly noticed, for growing into a woman as she was, she found that all things were new to her. And one sunny afternoon, as she sat with her maidens on the lawn by the ramparts of Emain Macha, high above the clustering houses that climbed the hill below, Deirdre saw a sight that struck her to the heart.

Striding down the dusty road that led away from the fortress was a magnificent man. He was not a craggy, secret, staring man like the King. He was taller than all the warriors of the fortress; his hair shone black, glittering in the sunlight like a raven's wing, and even from a distance, Deirdre could see

the blue of his eyes. Two men paced beside him. All three were singing, and the song they sang had the flutelike sweetness of the mistle thrush and the soaring gaiety of the skylark. The farmers in the fields paused and listened and smiled as the young men passed by; for they were the sons of Usnech, beloved in that province for their valor and their merry, open hearted natures. The tallest was Naoise; his brothers were Ainle and Ardan.

Deirdre rose and followed them. She ran along the road, calling after them, and although his brothers urged him away, Naoise paused and turned.

His fate had come upon him. Starbright, of a beauty that filled him with joy and sadness both at once, Deirdre stood before Naoise. There and then she captured his entire heart. His brothers saw this and warned him of the harm that would come if he took the woman the King had chosen, but Naoise cared nothing for the dishonor. Unable to move him, his brothers joined him, for the sons of Usnech, fiercely loyal, always acted together. That night

they took Deirdre away. Conchobar ordered that they be followed as soon as he learned of his loss. For months he tracked them through the provinces of Ireland, but the sons of Usnech were too swift for the King. At length, word came that they had taken Deirdre across the sea to Scotland, where the brothers fought for the Scots King, and Conchobar, defeated by distance, gave up the chase. Although he ceased to speak of vengeance as the years went by, Conchobar did not forget the woman, and the wound to his pride continued to fester.

Among his warriors, the memory of Deirdre soon faded, for she was but a maid who had been only briefly with them. The loss of the sons of Usnech was a lasting sorrow, however. They were loved for their bravery and for their sunny natures. Thus when Conchobar announced that he had forgiven the three, his Red Branch knights were filled with gladness, although some of them wondered at the ways of the King's mind.

Indeed, a thoughtful few suspected Conchobar, who was a guileful man. The King announced that the sons of Usnech were bound by a *geis:* They could leave Scotland only under the protection of the King's greatest warriors, Conall of the Victories and Cuchulain, or of Conchobar's kinsman, Fergus. No one had heard of this *geis;* it seemed clear that Conchobar had plans the warriors knew nothing about. Conall and Cuchulain refused to take part and left Emain Macha. Fergus trusted his nephew the King, however, and with his own two sons sailed for Scotland.

They landed at Loch Eitch in the west and found the houses that the sons of Usnech had built and saw Deirdre happy as she was then. Naoise and his brothers greeted Fergus joyfully, longing for their homeland and for the company of the Red Branch knights. Fergus pledged their safe

passage, but Deirdre wept when they sailed, and the lament she sang on shipboard for Scotland – for the wooded harbors, for the bird song echoing in the branches, for the clear sea washing the beaches, for the joy she had had there – drifted sadly over the wrinkling sea. When they landed in Ulster, Fergus and the sons of Usnech were deaf to the omens that marked their journey – to the eerie hooting of the tawny owl and the rare, chill song of swans on the Moyne. But Deirdre heard.

And, feeling her fate come upon her, she recognized the first bad thing for what it was: They lost the guardianship of Fergus soon after they disembarked. A lord of Ulster – a close companion of the King – had a feast waiting at his hall and he summoned Fergus to it. Fergus, like many of royal blood, was bound by the *geis* that he could not refuse a feast. He hesitated, red with anger and suspecting Conchobar's trickery – this bond conflicted with his pledge for the safety of the sons of Usnech. But at length he submitted to the bond and sent Deirdre

and the sons of Usnech on to Emain Macha in the care of his two sons, charging them to uphold his pledge.

And Deirdre knew the next bad thing when she heard of it: When the four arrived at Emain Macha, they – with Fergus' sons – were lodged not in the King's house but in the House of the Red Branch. The King did not appear – and Deirdre's childhood companion, Levarcham, warned them of Conchobar's treachery. Later, one of the King's men came and stared at

*When Deirdre returned to Ulster, King Conchobar betrayed his promise of safety.*
*He commanded an illusion of the sea to surround her protectors, so that they*
*dropped their swords and died in battle. Deirdre was left to the King.*

Deirdre through a window. And that night the six, imprisoned in the House of the Red Branch, heard shouting and smelled the acrid beginnings of fire. Conchobar's people were putting the house to the torch. The sons of Usnech leaped for their swords and fighting began. Such was Conchobar's guile and lying that some of his knights fought against the sons of Usnech and some for them. One of Fergus' sons defended the prisoners; the other was seduced by the King with the promise of land. All night long, while the fire raged,

the warriors of Ulster fought and died.

The sons of Usnech kept Deirdre safe and themselves alive until dawn. When the light broke at last, they linked their shields and, with Deirdre hidden behind them, burst through the doors of the Red Branch House and made for freedom.

But the doors opened into the depths of the sea. Cold salt water swept around them. Drowning, they dropped their shields and swords to swim upward, pushing toward the air.

Then the waves trembled and faded, and the weaponless men found themselves in the grip of Conchobar's guards. The engulfing water had been no more than illusion, conjured by Cathbad to stop the fighting after Conchobar promised that the sons of Usnech would get no harm from him. He had lied. He had the brothers killed—by a mercenary from Norway, because no man of Ulster would slay the sons of Usnech. The sword that killed them beheaded them all at one blow, so that none need see his brother die. As for Deirdre, the bearer of bad fate, there were differing accounts of her end. Some said she died at once, drinking the blood from the necks of the sons of Usnech. But others said that she wandered alone, mad with grief for Naoise, until she came to the

*Bereft of her beloved companions, Deirdre wished for life no longer. With a knife, she stabbed herself. She threw the weapon into the sea, that no one should bear the blame for her death.*

shores of the sea. She took a knife from a carpenter who was working there and stabbed herself to death.

And as for Fergus, when he at last arrived at Emain Macha and found that his pledge of safety had been broken by the King, he took revenge. With his men—and with Conchobar's son beside him—he burned the fortress to the ground. Then he and his company left Ulster forever and gave their service to Conchobar's enemy, Maeve of Connacht. So Fergus became a traitor because of the principles of honor. One wrong—Conchobar's deceit—forced a choice between two other wrongs, for had Fergus been with the sons of Usnech instead of honoring the bonds of his *geis*, Conchobar would not have dared to murder them. And the wizard Cathbad, enraged at Conchobar's lying, set this curse on the King: that none of his progeny should ever sit on the throne of Ulster.

None did: Conchobar's sons died childless in his own lifetime. The fortress at Emain Macha was restored and the Red Branch knights were reunited to fight in the endless wars against other Irish provinces. But when, in those cycles of vengeance, the champion Cuchulain died, the power of Ulster deteriorated. For centuries, it and the other Irish provinces were racked by petty wars, invasions and rebellions. At last, however, long after Cuchulain's death, order was restored by a race of powerful kings, who carved out a province for themselves—called Meath, or "the Middle," because it was at the very center of the country—and commanded the fealty of the lords of every Irish province.

The most magnificent of these High Kings was Cormac Mac Art, and his was the reign in which the brotherhood known as the Fianna reached its zenith. Founded during the reign of Cormac's grandfather, the Fianna was an army of men who were peace-keepers when the land was quiet and soldiers in times of war. They roamed throughout Ireland; in the summer they

lived in the open, in the winter they were quartered with the people.

As warriors they formed an elite, and those who wished to join their ranks had to pass a formidable battery of tests. The first prerequisite was mastery of Irish poetry, but this was child's play compared with the trials of valor and skill that the Fianna imposed. The candidate had, among other things, to stand knee-deep in a trench and with a shield and hazel wand protect himself from the javelins of nine warriors; he had to survive unwounded a chase through a thick wood and run so agilely that no braid of his hair—the Fianna plaited their long locks—could be loosened at the end. And during this chase he had to, without hesitating, jump branches as high as his forehead and duck under those no higher than his knee. At no time could he display the slightest fear.

If he survived the trials, he joined a band of brothers whose deeds became the stuff of legend. In Cormac's time, they were led by the chieftain Finn Mac Cumal, whose name glittered with glories. It was said that while still a boy he slew a night creature that each year burned the High King's fortress at Tara, that he had tasted a magic salmon and thus acquired a wizard's powers, that he excelled swallows in speed and dolphins at swimming, that water giv-

en from his cupped hands saved the dying. It was said of Finn that if his deadliest enemy and his son came before him for arbitration of a quarrel, the enemy need not fear unfair judgment. And he was as famed for his generosity as for his justness.

Finn was no Conchobar and his warriors were milder men than those of the Red Branch. Yet they were bound by the same conflicting rules of honor as Conchobar's knights. And when people made use of these codes for their own ends, the result was dishonor. Such a tragedy touched even Finn near the end of his life.

In the winter of his years, Finn desired a bride to warm him. He had been married before—to the offspring of kings and to a woman of the fairy people—but these wives were gone. The woman he chose now was auburn-haired Grainne, daughter of the High King, Cormac Mac Art. She was a proud and headstrong maid, who had refused a dozen fine matches. But when Cormac told her of Finn's offer, she acquiesced, albeit with indifference. She said words to the effect that if the leader of the Fianna was good enough for the

High King, he was good enough for her.

So with his band of heroes, Finn left his stronghold on the Hill of Allen, a limestone peak towering over the Leinster wetlands, and journeyed to the High King's fortress at Tara for the wedding feast.

A feasting at Tara then was a time of marvels. Five great roads led to the grassy hill where the fortress stood, its lime-washed double ramparts shining white across the surrounding plain. Within the walls were the King's round palaces; his houses for hostages and for troops; his feather-covered *greenan*, a pleasance built for Grainne and her ladies; and his twelve-doored banqueting hall, more than seven hundred feet long and made of carved and painted timber. There, the warriors' shields were hung so that each man might be seated before his own. The guests were summoned by golden trumpets, and harpers played to them as they ate.

Grainne sat with her father and Finn, now her husband, at the high table and contemplated the men of the Fianna. There were so many, such a spectacle of blue eyes and bronzed skin and braided hair, such an aura of strength and vigor and merriment, that it was hard to tell them apart. There was Finn's son Oisin, the sweet singer, and his grandson Oscar, commander of a battalion that had never retreated. Slender Caolite was there, famed for his fleetness. One-eyed Goll was there, a fierce fighter; and Conan, full of bragging idiocies, but faithful.

But the man Grainne's eyes lingered on was none of these. She watched a splendid warrior—young, not gray-haired like her husband—with a cap low on his brow. This was Diarmuid. He had journeyed under the sea once and killed a sorcerer who had ensnared the Fianna. He was famed for his valor and his insouciance. A fate awaited him, an enchanted boar that had been made to avenge a murder Diarmuid's father had done; but the boar was far away, and Diarmuid seemed unaware of the menace.

As Grainne watched Diarmuid, all the while making conversation with her grave husband, a fight broke out among the hounds in the hall. Diarmuid leaped up and pulled the animals apart, and in doing so he lost the cap he wore to hide a small mark—set on his forehead by an enchantress—that was said to entrance any woman who looked on it. Grainne saw the mark. Pride, honor and duty fled from her heart.

She did not hesitate. From her *ciorbolg*—the small bag in which women carried their ivory combs—she drew a sleeping draught. She slipped the powder into a wine cup and offered the wine to each of the guests. Only Diarmuid was offered no wine.

In moments, every guest but Diarmuid was slumped over the table. As Diarmuid viewed the scene in surprise, Grainne approached him. She smiled and said calmly, "Take me from this place tonight."

Appalled at the invitation to betray his leader and his honor, Diarmuid refused. Grainne was not disturbed. She looked down modestly, and when she looked up again, iron will shone from her eyes.

"I place you under a *geis* to take me away tonight," she said, and left the hall.

His companions began to wake and Diarmuid approached the two who were

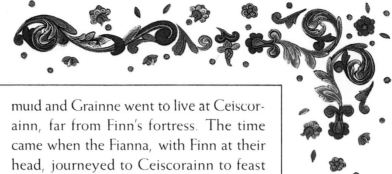

his closest friends. He told them of the bond Grainne had placed on him and of his dilemma; but both said the *geis* must be obeyed. Diarmuid put the question to Finn himself, phrasing it theoretically. Finn raised his brows in surprise.

"A *geis* must be followed," he said.

And so in the night, shamefully, like the thief he had become, Diarmid left Tara with Grainne and made for the wilderness.

Years of flight followed. Wise in its ways, Diarmuid followed the rules: The couple never sheltered in a tree with only one trunk or in a cave with only one opening. They never ate where they cooked, never slept where they ate and never slept in one place the night through. To retrieve what he could of his honor, Diarmuid refused to touch Grainne; and at night he left outside their camp a loaf of unbroken bread to signify that Finn's wife remained a virgin. But Grainne had a nature fired by a grand passion; she waited.

Finn, as skilled as Diarmuid in flight and pursuit, tracked the pair easily. He saw the bread and knew its meaning but still he followed. His son and grandson tried to call him off: As he himself had said, a *geis* must be obeyed, and Diarmuid was obeying as honorably as he could. But the pair had shamed the old man, and he could not heed his kin. He fought Diarmuid when he could, but the younger man always escaped; sometimes, it was said, with aid from the other world.

The passionate will cannot be resisted forever; at last Diarmuid took Grainne for his own and ceased to leave the unbroken loaf outside his camp. But in the end, Finn was persuaded to make his peace. Diar-

muid and Grainne went to live at Ceiscorainn, far from Finn's fortress. The time came when the Fianna, with Finn at their head, journeyed to Ceiscorainn to feast with them and seal the peace.

In the small hours of the morning after they arrived, Diarmuid woke to the baying of a hound a mile away on Benbulben. He rose and armed himself. Grainne drowsily tried to stop him, but he paid no mind. He fetched his own hounds and made off across the valley and up the steep slopes of the ben. Near the crest, in the morning mists, a figure stood alone. It was Finn.

"Some of us came out after midnight," Finn said. "A hound caught the scent of a boar. We've lost it now; best leave it."

For a hero, the fated end was ineluctable: a challenge that, even with the certainty of defeat, must be accepted. Diarmuid had a *geis* not to hunt boar, because of the beast that was his end. He knew that it was this boar and that its presence was Finn's doing. He knew that his happiness with Grainne was no more than an interlude before the tightening of the coil that had been shaped years before at Tara. The important thing now was to die, as he had failed to live, with honor.

Thudding hoofbeats preceded the eruption of the boar into the clearing where they stood. Diarmuid's hounds fled when they saw the murderous eyes and curving tusks of the enormous animal. But it was Diarmuid the boar wanted. While Finn watched impassively, the young man cast a spear; it struck between the animal's eyes and bounced off the

At the feast of her wedding to Finn Mac Cumal, Grainne of Ireland was smitten by the beauty of Finn's knight Diarmuid. With a magic drink, she drugged the wedding guests; with magic oaths, she bound Diarmuid to flee with her and so betray his duty to Finn.

thick skull. The boar charged. Diarmuid withstood the onslaught and brought his sword down on the creature's neck, but the blade shattered. Locked together, man and beast struggled; the boar dragged Diarmuid across the grass for endless moments until at last, in a welter of blood, both were still. Diarmuid lay dying where he had fallen, his body torn open by the yellow tusks. The boar was dead; Diarmuid's sword hilt had smashed its head.

Finn heard shouts as the men of the Fianna climbed the ben, drawn by the noise of the battle. He stood over Diarmuid, a wry smile played about his lips:

"You are not so beautiful as you once were, Diarmuid," he said.

Finn's grandson Oscar heard and said angrily, "Give him his life back." For all knew that water from Finn's hands would save a dying man. Finn shook his head.

"Give him his life," said Oscar again.

"For the deeds I did for you when I was with the Fianna," said Diarmuid with difficulty, "give me my life now."

Slowly Finn walked over to a small spring. He filled his hands with the cold water, and while his grandson watched, he walked slowly back to where Diarmuid lay. But as he approached, his lips tightened with the memory of Grainne, and the water trickled through his fingers.

Again Oscar spoke. Again Finn got water. Again he let it trickle away.

His grandson called on Finn's honor, and knowing he must, Finn brought water a third time and held it to Diarmuid's lips.

But Diarmuid was already dead.

So in the end the tragedy and the glory were Diarmuid's. Caught by the chains of honor, he met with courage the death he knew fate held in store. At the last, urged by his grandson, Finn made the move that saved his name.

And his name shone steadily through long, dark centuries. The Fianna, as the years passed, grew mighty, and arrogant in their might. Loyal only to their brotherhood, they rebelled against the High King and were finally destroyed.

But just as people said Cuchulain rode the skies in his battle chariot many years after his death, they said the best and brightest of the Fianna survived. With Finn they slept an enchanted sleep in a cave hidden from mortal eyes, waiting for the time when Ireland should need them and Finn would again awake. ᧤

The warrior was a woman. Sigurd had awakened her from a magical sleep.

# Treachery of the Nibelungs

Glory and treachery, early death and endless sorrow — these were the threads that Scandinavian poets wove into songs about Sigurd, the last of Denmark's Volsung clan. The Volsungs were a race of heroes descended from the gods. True to his high lineage, Sigurd had barely reached manhood when he slew a dragon that stood baleful watch over a treasure hoard. He capped the conquest by bathing in the beast's blood. This made his flesh invulnerable, save for one place on his shoulder where a linden leaf had fallen and covered his skin while he took the gruesome bath.

After his encounter with the dragon, Sigurd rode south in search of new adventure. Before many days passed, he spied a pillar of smoke rising from a mountain peak and, eager to know the cause, guided his horse Greyfell up the slope. As he neared the summit, he saw that the mountain itself burned: The peak was ringed with ramparts of fire.

Sigurd spurred his horse straight toward the flame, and Greyfell went willingly, hoofs hammering on the burning coals as if on cold pebbles. As they entered the fire, it subsided to flickering tongues of flame and then died to ashes. Sigurd saw

*The flames sprang up around Brynhild, guarding her until Sigurd should claim her again.*

what it had shielded: a stone bier, and on the bier, the gold-clad body of a warrior.

Dismounting, he removed the warrior's helmet. A wealth of golden hair tumbled out, framing a sternly beautiful face. He cut the thongs that held the glittering breastplate. The warrior was a woman. Moreover, she was alive: Sigurd had evidently awakened her from a magical sleep.

For a moment, the woman gazed gravely up at him. Then, with the litheness of the battle-trained, she sprang to her feet and stood before him. She spoke, and Sigurd's heart leaped within his breast. Sigurd had breached the fire fortress, the woman warrior said, and only the bravest of mortals could do so. She was therefore his.

This woman was a hero's prize indeed, as Sigurd recognized when she told him her name: Brynhild. She was a Valkyrie—one of the heroic troop of near-goddesses who rode the clouds high above a battlefield, choosing the warriors who would perish in glory. Once, however, she had chosen a warrior before his appointed time, and she had been condemned to live among humankind and learn its sorrows. But because she was a Valkyrie, she was sent into a deep sleep, secure in the fire fortress, so that only the greatest of heroes—he who braved the flames—should have her.

For a time—none knew how long—Sigurd and Brynhild talked together, and at last they pledged their troth. In token of his vow, Sigurd gave the Valkyrie a ring that he had taken from the dragon's hoard; she gave him runic charms to keep him high-hearted and strengthen his sword. Then the mortal rode

*The Nibelung Queen Grimhild offered Sigurd a cup of wine tainted by her dark arts.*

away to find a king to serve—and deeds to do to make him worthy of this woman of the clouds. Behind him, the Valkyrie sank once more onto her bier. The flames sprang up, guarding her until Sigurd should claim her again.

Sigurd traveled long months through the world, finally reaching the land of the Nibelungs, a forest tribe ruled by a King called Giuki. Sigurd's air of honor and courage won him entrance to the King's hall, and his tale of dragon gold and of his Valkyrie won him the attention of the Queen. Grimhild was her name; she was a sorceress, and she was ruled only by ambition for her children.

As she listened to the warrior's tale, the thought came to her that he was a fitting match for her daughter Gudrun. At once she devised a way to achieve this end, offering the warrior a cup of wine tainted by her dark arts. Sigurd's mind clouded, and the memory of his battle maiden slipped away. Beside him stood Gudrun, tender and fair; his heart moved toward her.

Not many weeks passed before Sigurd married Gudrun, just as the sorceress had planned. Gudrun's family became his, and Sigurd was as a brother to her brothers—to Guttorm and Hogni and especially to Gunnar, the eldest and the best. Sigurd and Gunnar hunted together and went to war together, and they swore eternal friendship.

Then Grimhild, who watched all her children's doings closely, was ready to make her second match. She sent her son Gunnar to woo Brynhild, finest of maidens, and she sent Sigurd to aid him. Sigurd, his mind still held by the sorceress's magic, the memory of his promise gone, was eager to help

*Dishonored, Brynhild appealed for vengeance to the Nibelung warrior Hogni.*

his companion and brother, in this matter as in all others.

The two young men traveled to Brynhild's enchanted mountain. Sigurd held back while Gunnar charged the fire fortress. Gunnar's horse refused to breach the ring of flames. Then Gunnar tried again with Sigurd's horse, but Greyfell would move for no rider other than Sigurd.

In the end, they used a ruse—as Grimhild no doubt had anticipated would be necessary, for she had sent with them the magic that made it. With the aid of spells, the young men exchanged shape; in the guise of Gunnar, Sigurd charged the flames and approached the Valkryie. Brynhild found a stranger by her bier. She believed then that Sigurd must be dead, for only the greatest warrior in the world could breach her wall of flame. This man had clearly taken Sigurd's place in honor and valor. Grieving, she gave him her golden ring and agreed that, as her own fate demanded, she would marry him.

Strife came into the family of the Nibelung Kings at the wedding feast of its eldest son. Beside Gunnar and Brynhild in the hall sat Sigurd with his wife, Gudrun, and Gudrun wore upon her hand the golden ring of the dragon hoard. Brynhild stared. It was the very same Sigurd she had loved, tall, handsome, with a broad brow and hair like curled copper. He met her eyes and looked away.

In the days that followed, the women quarreled. Gudrun had seen the Valkyrie's look of longing for her husband, and she did not like it. She told Brynhild what Sigurd had said secretly (and innocently, having lost all memory of his vow to Brynhild): He had wooed Brynhild for Gunnar. Gudrun

*Into the only vulnerable spot on Sigurd's body plunged Hogni's treacherous spear.*

showed the golden ring that Sigurd had kept as his reward and given to her, his wife, to wear.

Then Brynhild turned away from her husband, Gunnar, with contempt. It was not he who had ridden through the ring of flames, and the trick he had used brought shame to her. She spoke against Sigurd and demanded that Gunnar kill him to retrieve his own lost honor.

But Gunnar would not do it. Sigurd, he said, was his blood brother. Brynhild appealed—as was her right—to Gunnar's younger brother Hogni, who had a spiteful nature and a taste for treachery. He took on the task. He began with Sigurd's wife and contrived, with smooth words and protestations of anxiety for Sigurd's safety, to make that loose-tongued woman reveal to him the one vulnerability that Sigurd had—the spot on his shoulder that the linden leaf had covered.

With that knowledge, the task of killing Sigurd was easy. Hogni went hunting with him one day, deep in the German forests, and watched while Sigurd brought down the prey. Hot and thirsty, the two men raced for a spring to bathe and drink, and Sigurd won the race. He rose from the water, wet and laughing, his back to Hogni. Hogni thrust a spear at his shoulder; the blade entered and plunged deep.

Thus died Sigurd. Brynhild, wild with grief, flung herself on his funeral pyre and gave herself to the flame that she might have him for eternity. As for Hogni and the rest of the Nibelung brood, they died years later, tricked into fighting one another by Gudrun, who from the moment of Sigurd's death lived only for vengeance.

# Chapter Three

# Brotherhood of the Round Table

One time, in the age of Britain's shining glory, when King Arthur wore the crown, two mounted knights clashed in single combat. They battled for the sakes of two women, and the prize they sought was a hawk.

The adventure began in this fashion: A Breton knight of Arthur's court, Erec, son of Lac, rode out one fine spring morning in attendance on Arthur's Queen while she hunted with her ladies in the western forests. In the course of the hunt, an astonishing event occurred. A knight clad in gold and blue appeared among the trees, and there was a lady beside him. The pair was accompanied by a squat dwarf who, while the mortal couple watched impassively, hurled insults at the Queen and — when Sir Erec intervened — at Erec himself. The dwarf advanced and struck the Queen's knight across the face with a knotted scourge. Then, with a malevolent leer from the dwarf, a haughty laugh from the knight and a faint smile from the lady, the curious trio wheeled their horses and vanished into the forest.

Sir Erec sent the Queen and her ladies to safety under the escort of his squire. Then he himself turned and, unarmed save for his sword and hunting bow, rode after the strangers, resolved on revenge.

He rode for hours on a twisting, tree-shrouded track until the forest gave way to rolling fields and shadowy hills. The track led through this unfamiliar country to a fortress; under its looming walls and towers were clustered the slate-tiled roofs of a large town. Far ahead on the road Sir Erec saw three small mounted figures, one clad in gold, nearing the town gates. He spurred his horse and followed them.

Within the gates, the streets of the town were crowded, restlessly eddying with a holiday throng. Sir Erec's quarry was nowhere to be seen. His horse picked its way carefully over the cobblestones toward the center of the town; Sir Erec ignored the appraising glances cast his way. Court ladies in silvery velvets watched him from under modestly lowered lashes; red-faced matrons, their heads swathed in linen wimples, smiled broadly; scarlet-robed trollops called out open invitations. Oth-

er people watched the young knight, too: cloaked riders with falcons on their wrists, tonsured friars in robes of gray and black, rubicund yeomen, peddlers, tinkers, beggars and thieves.

Nobody intercepted him, however, and he eventually arrived at the heart of the town – a long grass-covered jousting field. At its verge was a tall pole, and perched on the boss that crowned it was a sparrow hawk whose folded wings were the gray of the roof tiles and whose breast was boldly barred with rufous brown. The bird's head was hidden under a green feathered hood; its legs were cuffed by gold-belled jesses attached to a leash of Spanish leather; and thus elegantly blinded and shackled, the fierce and beautiful creature waited quietly on its perch.

Sir Erec looked around to find his gaze met by a grave old man, a knight by his bearing, who stood at the edge of the field. Beside his tall, somber figure stood a young woman, plainly dressed in white linen but of such fairness that Sir Erec's breath caught in his throat and his hands tightened on the reins. His horse took an uncertain step backward, recalling him to himself, and he saluted the stranger courteously. The old man bowed. Sir Erec, dismounting, joined him and tried not to stare at his fair young companion.

Like most of Arthur's knights, Sir Erec had an engaging, easy demeanor, and it was not long before the old man told him all he wished to know and offered the hospitality owed to honorable strangers. The town's holiday, he said, was the celebration of a rite. Once each year, knights jousted there in honor of their ladies, to determine which was the fairest. To the victor went the sparrow hawk, the wind rider whose strength and perfect beauty could be matched only by the best of women. For the last two years, the victor had been a knight named Yder, an aging, arrogant hulk of a man whose proud lady had claimed the hawk each spring; none dared challenge him any longer. Sir Yder wore arms of gold and azure, and when Sir Erec heard this, his lips tightened; he knew he had found the man he sought.

He said little at the time, however. He walked with the old man and his daughter – for such was the fair young woman – to the house they had in the town. He saw his horse safely stabled and at dinner learned something of his hosts. The old man was a landowner who had sold his lands to pay for war ventures. He no longer fought: Age and poverty prevented it. His daughter, who was called Enide, was a woman without a dowry, and a penniless woman, no matter how beautiful and good, had a hard lot in those days.

Sir Erec cared nothing for that. He had seen Enide and he loved her. Himself the son of a mighty prince, he had no need of a dowry, and so he told his host. After the wine had gone around and the fire had faded to glowing embers, he said thoughtfully, "I would challenge Yder. I do not like that knight. And I will fight him in the lady's name, if she will have me, for she is the fairest maiden that ever I saw."

Enide blushed delicately; she glanced at her father, and with a smile, he nodded. A valorous prince was a fine match indeed.

Thus easily, the thing was done—or at least agreed upon. The battle still remained, and Yder was known as a warrior who gave no quarter.

In the silver dawn of the following day, Enide armed Sir Erec in her own father's harness, for the knight had brought none of his own. Over a woolen shirt and breeches, he wore an acton, a leather tunic that protected him from the bite of his armor: A blow on chain mail could drive the links into a man's flesh. A hauberk—a thirty-pound coat of mail—went over that. On his head, he wore a leather cap to ease the pressure of his helmet. This burnished helmet weighed twenty-five pounds; it was adorned with yellow ribbons, tied there by Enide as a sign of her favor.

Mounted on his own tall stallion, Sir Erec rode to the field to challenge Yder. Behind him rode Enide on a pretty palfrey, and the holiday crowd ceased its raucous chatter at the sweet sight of her.

Sir Yder was waiting. He laughed at Sir Erec's claim for Enide's beauty. He sneered at Erec's challenge, calling the younger knight a coward and a lily-faced stripling. He ceased to sneer, however, when Sir Erec shouted execration upon his valor. With a grim smile, Yder signaled to the heralds of the town.

Pushings and heavings and angry commands at last cleared the field for the antagonists. A ritual began, executed according to the strictest rules of chivalry, which were known not only to the participants but to every member of the crowd. Insults were the conventional preliminary. Had Erec and Yder been devoted brothers, they still would have taunted each other.

And when the fighting started, ritual dictated the pace, the sequence of events, the pauses, the weapons—everything, in fact, but the outcome. Jousting—mounted battle with lances—opened the contest. Facing each other across a field hundreds of feet long, the knights donned their helmets, and at a signal from the heralds, each charged straight at the other. Riding without reins to leave his hands free—the horses responded to knee signals—each man held his shield athwart his body and his lance pointed ahead with a slight deflection toward his opponent. The best fighters struck lance point to midshield, but rare was the knight who could so accurately manipulate a point that floated twice a man's length ahead of him while his mount's thundering pace rocked him in the saddle. With an earsplitting crash, Erec and Yder struck. Both lances shattered at impact on the shields and the force threw both men to the ground.

The second stage of the tourney began. Their swords drawn, their movements encumbered by the weight of their armor, the two circled slowly, chain mail chinking and jingling. Then they closed in. Turn and turn about, the great blades crashed down deafeningly on helm and shield and hauberk. Constricted by their trappings, both striker and victim took minutes to recover from each blow, while blots of their blood browned in the dusty grass. Theirs was a long and ponderous dance, quite possibly one of death.

Hours passed. Excitement in the crowd ebbed and flowed as, again and again, a

*When Arthur was King, gallant knights fought in honor of their ladies. And so it was that Sir Erec of the Round Table engaged in a mighty joust for the fair Enide and won a prize for her—a splendid little hunting hawk.*

kill seemed imminent and was evaded. At opposite sides of the field, Enide and Yder's lady sat on their palfreys, motionless as statues except for the fluttering of their veils in the breeze. On its high perch, the sparrow hawk, too, was quiet. The shadows lengthened. Yder, the defender, called for a rest.

The two men paused, leaning on the hilts of their swords and panting for breath. Sir Erec turned his head and saw, framed by the slits in his visor, the white figure of Enide, sitting on the small gray horse. Heartened, he turned back to Yder.

"Dog," he said, "the time has come to end your folly."

So the last stage of the fight began. Blades ringing, the men sought out the chinks and gashes in each other's armor: A lunge that was not well parried could hook in a seam of a hauberk and slip into the flesh—or penetrate the visor and blind a knight. A careless turn sent blood down Yder's arm; the gold and azure tunic that he wore was spattered with it.

Yder was growing tired; he lurched like a drunkard, and Erec, slighter but younger, moved in. His sword smashed down on Yder's helm and the knight hesitated, swaying where he stood. A second blow split the helmet and slashed bloodily into the skull. Yder tottered; then, with a clang of metal, he crashed to the ground.

Swift as a hound with a hare, Erec was beside him, wrenching the shattered ventail of the helm to expose Sir Yder's throat. But the older man was not prepared to die. Muffled by the remains of the helm, his voice sounded on the field: "I yield to your mercy," he cried. "My sword is yours. And the hawk to your lady."

But there was more to the surrender. Yder bound himself and his lady and his loathsome dwarf to journey to Arthur's court and accept whatever punishment the Queen chose for the insult he had given her. After that he was left alone until his people came to take him home, for the crowd, silent in the last long moments of the fight, surged around Sir Erec. They pulled his battered helmet from his head and, cheering, led him to his lady.

They cheered when Sir Erec took the sparrow hawk from its perch and passed it

to Enide's hand. The bird, aloof through all the hours of bloodshed, stepped willingly onto her glove and roused and settled its feathers. It seemed content there, as if it had found a fellow spirit, loftily distant from the conflicts of men.

Sir Erec was a warrior who lived in a brave new world. Centuries had passed since the wild hunting days of the Irish Fianna, and even longer since Cuchulain had died in glory. For decades, Britain, or Logres as it was called, had been at peace, guided by the steady hand of Arthur.

The King was old now, but his vigor was undiminished and the deeds of his youth still shone around him in a nimbus of bright magic. His very birth, like that of earlier heroes, had been brought about by enchantment, as even the youngest page at court knew. Long years before, when England was torn by civil strife and battered by enemies from across the sea, the archenchanter Merlin had changed the shape of the reigning King, Uther Pendragon, to that of one of his lords, Gorlois of Cornwall. The spell had lasted for one night only, and in that night, at the windy fortress of Tintagel in Cornwall, Uther had fathered a son upon Gorlois's wife, Igraine. The child was Arthur, and because the times were troublous, Merlin had hidden the infant until he should be ready to claim his throne when Uther died.

That happened fourteen years later, and Merlin took the youth to London. There, before the eyes of the chief lords of England, Arthur pulled from a stone a ceremonial sword that none but the rightful king could move. When its jeweled hilt slid into his hand, Arthur stepped into his inheritance, with Merlin at his side.

The young King had to fight for his throne. It took him years to subdue the various British factions and defend his land against his enemies abroad. But his was a fine spirit—and he had the aid of Merlin. It was Merlin who led Arthur to his battle sword, Excalibur, the weapon forged by fairy people in a kingdom under a lake. Its blade was invincible; its scabbard healed any wound it touched; and with Excalibur, Arthur united his realm.

It was Merlin, too, who ordered the creation of the Round Table, at least according to some chroniclers. It was said that he had the table built for the knights of Arthur's father. Its shape reflected eternal perfection because it had no beginning and no end; because the table was circular, no one of the knights seated there could take precedence over another. Except for one, that is: The table had a place called the Siege Perilous, or dangerous seat, which could be claimed only by the greatest knight in the world, whose mettle would be proved, said one of Merlin's prophecies, by the greatest of quests.

The seat remained unoccupied. Just before he died, Uther gave the table to King Leodegran of Cornwall, and it became part of the dowry of Leodegran's daughter, the loveliest princess of her day, when she married Arthur. Her name was Guinevere, and she brought to her husband not only the Round Table, the object that signified the perfect unity of his company of knights, but also the seeds of something that would destroy that brotherhood.

## None but the brave deserved the fair

In the age of chivalry, people liked to tell tales of the winning of fair women, and when they sang of valiant lovers, they sang of Art of Ireland.

He was the son of a High King named Conn of the Hundred Battles and a warrior like his father. All alone, he made a quest to win a woman of Faerie. She was called Delvcaem of the Fair Shape and she was the unhappy prisoner of her parents. Her mother, it was said, was a sorceress who would die when Delvcaem wed, and therefore she kept the maiden shut away. And with her husband, Morgan, she murdered every suitor bold enough to venture near her fortress.

To gain Delvcaem, Art set sail on forbidden seas where mortals never went; he let the currents take him into the lands of Faerie. And as he neared her territory, the sorceress knew it. By her magic she threw obstacles into his path – witches and giants and poisonous toads.

Art slew them all and won his way to the fortress of the sorceress. It was ringed with bronze stakes, on each of which was impaled the head of a warrior who had tried to win Delvcaem. There was an empty stake, too, awaiting Art's own head.

But Art was a man without fear, and when the sorceress emerged in armor to challenge him to battle, he fought her willingly. And it was her head that ended up crowning the empty bronze stake. Then Art beheaded Delvcaem's father, Morgan.

When he had triumphed, Art took the waiting Delvcaem in his arms. In his valor he braved the sea once more. And, the storytellers said, magic helped the lovers. The waves caressed them as gently as a summer wind, to carry the pair safe home to Ireland.

But the sad end was many years away when Sir Erec left the Queen's side to find and fight Yder. In Sir Erec's time, Arthur's company was at the crest of its glory and his court was the finest in Christendom. The Round Table stood in the great hall of Camelot, Arthur's fortress, which some say was in Somerset and some in Cornwall. The finest champions in the world – sons of lords and kings and princes, unmatched in valor – had flocked to Arthur's side, for to serve him was the aim in life for any man of worth. Sir Gawain, staunchly faithful and the model of chivalry, was there then, carrying something of magic in his sunny nature, for his strength waxed from dawn until noon and waned as the sun descended. With him were kindly Sir Percival; plodding, diligent Sir Bors; irascible and boastful Sir Kay; Sir Gareth, both brave

and modest; Sir Palomides the Saracen; Sir Dinadan, always swearing that discretion was the better part of valor, and yet always courageous; and the acknowledged champion, Sir Lancelot. They were 150 in all at the height of Arthur's reign.

In later, safer, duller times, it is difficult to imagine the splendor of Camelot. High on its grassy hill the castle rose, its battlements tier upon tier of golden stone, its clustering towers crowned with the fluttering standards of the King. Within the walls was a city of chivalry. There were barracks for soldiers, forges and armories for their weapons, stables and saddleries for their horses, and mews for their hawks. All of these were crowded near the broad green jousting field, at a remove from the stately calm of the palace itself, with its great halls, its tapestried chambers, its library and treasury and chapel, its maze of walled, flower-bright gardens.

**C**amelot sheltered a society of warriors, but time had wrought dramatic changes in the character of the knight. He had become chivalrous. The word literally means only that he was a horseman. Equipped with powerful destriers, high, velvet-covered wooden saddles and stirrups—which were invented in Asia and unknown in Europe in the Irish heroes' time—a warrior could fight securely from horseback, gaining ferocious mobility thereby.

The chevalier's childhood was spent in training for this demanding pursuit. At the age of seven, boys of good birth were taken from their families and sent to live as pages in noble households, where they waited on adults and learned the arts of the hunt and of war. Throughout the castle of Camelot—in the great hall, in the Queen's solar, in the stables with the grooms, in the mews with the falconers, in the kennels with the dogboys—could be seen the little figures of the royal pages, anonymous, often lonely and usually bone weary. It took years to train the mind and muscles to the discipline of sword and saddle and the intricacies of the lance.

At fourteen, promising pages became squires, entitled to wear helmets and spurs and serve as apprentices and servants to knights in the field. If all went well, they were themselves knighted at twenty-one.

But chivalry implied much more than its literal meaning. Under its aegis, the raw ethics of ancient heroism had mellowed and matured. The wild impulses of the heroes of Cuchulain's age had been refined by a new code, which molded instinct into a repertoire of artifice, a code that pages and squires absorbed as they grew.

A knight of Arthur's company was not only a warrior, bound by the rules of warriors' honor, but also a protector of the weak and of the unfortunate. He never could refuse an appeal for aid. He was required to fight with a semblance of humaneness: He could never intentionally harm his opponent's horse, for instance. No dueling knight, unless it was agreed that the contest continue to the death, could ignore an opponent's cry for mercy, and the fiercest duels sometimes ended with the victor ripping strips from his tunic to bind his victim's wounds.

Forms and rules of behavior proliferated, on the field and in the hall. Especially in the hall, for the women who presided there had acquired a new and curious status, at least in theory. Their ancestresses had been warriors, and queens in their own right—or victims or lovers or simply bedmates—but these women were set on pedestals as idols and as inspiration for the knights of the court. Women, of course, were not transformed by chivalry: Only the idea of woman was sanctified. Women loved, married, gave birth, worked, hunted, laughed and cried just as they always had, but that did not matter. For chivalrous knights, they were celestial ideals, imperious paragons to be worshipped from afar and honored by great deeds.

In some courts, this attitude was carried to absurd lengths, at least according to the troubadours. In the luxurious, sophisticated palaces of Provence, public trials were held by court ladies to judge the behavior of their admirers. And in Germany it was said that Ulrich, Count of Lichtenstein, wore out his horse with traveling and his body with fighting in the service of a lady whom he loved. She responded icily, refraining from comment on his victories and sending his messengers on their way. She was told once that Ulrich had lost a finger in a tournament; she made no answer until she heard that in fact the finger had merely received a cut. Then she sent a letter, savaging the knight for what she called his lie. When a messenger delivered this missive to Ulrich, he knelt without hesitation—as he always did on receipt of her words—and ordered the messenger to cut off the offending finger.

Ulrich was, of course, a case of history gone mad, a copybook example of male obeisance to a sacred image of femininity. At King Arthur's court, a mirror of chivalry, few would have sympathized with this self-humbling dotard, and not even the most callow of knights would have emulated him. Women were held high—much higher than they had been centuries before—but they were not lost in the clouds. They were sought after, fought over, loved and honored. And because in those times their honor reflected that of the men who protected them, they cherished valor and bestowed their smiles on the brave.

Thus Sir Erec found his bride while avenging the Queen's honor, as his own honor demanded, and won Enide through a display of valor and skill. They married; he retired with her to his own lands and there he remained for months in passionate seclusion. He did not show himself at court; he did not seek adventure. Whispers began, and laughter, and at last Enide herself warned Sir Erec that a hero's reputation faded like snowdrops if he abandoned himself to less demanding pleasures. If he would remain a hero, he must ride out and seek adventure once again. And so he did.

For the quest for adventure was essential to King Arthur's knights. Trained to battle, they were fully themselves only in battle, when every skill was brought into complete and violent play. They sought perfection in bravery time and time again.

They lived in a relatively peaceful age, however. The ceaseless petty wars that their ancestors had fought were no more.

## The dream of King Arthur

In the bright young years of his reign, King Arthur once set out on a hunt, during which he stopped to rest beside a forest pool. As he slept, he dreamed of horrors. Images of dragons swam in his dream, of griffins and other terrible creatures slaughtering his people. Worst of all was the Questing Beast, a ghastly serpent whose nostrils streamed noxious flame and whose voice was that of baying hounds. The creature drank from the clear water of the pool and vanished into shadow.

The King awoke much shaken. His dream was a stain spread across the hopes of his heart. And so it was, as Merlin the Enchanter advised him.

The Questing Beast was more than a mere dream. It was the loathsome spawn of a princess who had attempted to seduce her own brother and, when he refused her, had had the man eaten alive by dogs. Her punishment was this offspring, which roamed the world eternally, a perverse thing formed by perverse wishes.

And Arthur saw it because of perversity. Before he learned his mother's name – for he was reared in secret, far from her – he had lain with his mother's daughter, his half sister, Queen Morgause of Orkney. Morgause bore him a son, who one day would be England's downfall.

Thus Merlin told the King, so that through the glories of his life, Arthur saw the shadow of the future. He himself had fathered the man who would destroy all he had made.

*King Arthur sought a queen fit for a royal crown and found her in Guinevere, daughter of Leodegran of Cornwall. The dowry she brought was a magnificent one—one hundred noble knights and the Round Table of Uther Pendragon.*

The knights at court were never idle; there were always the diversions of the hunt and the formalized warfare of the tournament. But those were artifice, and thus it was the practice of Arthur's knights to ride out alone in search of adventure, to put themselves at risk and burnish their valor.

A knight would be absent, sometimes for years. And then one day his tattered standard would appear on the plain below the fortress at Camelot. His comrades on the battlements would see his battered form, as Gawain once was seen returning from a quest. In the words of the chronicler: "The knight sat on a tall horse, lean and bony. His hauberk was all rusty and his shield pierced in a dozen places and its color so fretted away that none could recognize the device thereon. And a right thick spear he bore in his hand."

He had found and won his battles and so could rest, for a time. And battles were easy to find. England was at peace, it was true, but the age was one of wonders, and the farther reaches of the island were thronged with mysteries. In the mountains to the north lived giants—huge, coarse cannibals. And where there was water in that well-watered land, there were the people of Faerie, enchanting and powerful, capricious and full of danger. In the depths of the forests that covered most of England, curiously wrought fountains were to be found, and their guardians were not mortal. Hidden beneath the still surfaces of mountain lakes were shimmering palaces and flowering fields, where knights could be trapped to languish forever.

Those who stood on the western shores of the island often saw—now appearing, now disappearing in the drifting mist of the Irish Sea—the crystal turrets of palaces that graced the peaks of enchanted isles. Beyond a bend in a forest road he thought he knew, the questing knight might come upon a watchtower, its windows empty as dead men's eyes; he might call a challenge, but the only answer he would get would be the rustling of the ivy as it stirred against the crumbling stones and the creaking of his saddle as his horse shifted anxiously under him. In the silence he would have a sense of ears that listened and eyes that watched, of elder intelligences quietly observing. Then he would have to enter the tower and face whatever lurked within and, with the wit of his brain and the strength and swiftness of his arm, prove his right to knighthood.

Tests of this sort came upon the knight unawares; he had only to ride out into the still-uncharted forests and cross a border he could not see to find himself pitted against the nameless forces of the other world. But also waiting, eternally vigilant, were enchantresses, dark counterparts of the ladies of Arthur's court, and their names were well known. Many knights, even Arthur himself, had succumbed to their magic at one time or another.

These dark ladies were as elusive as the play of light on water. They were both good and bad, both desiring and detesting mortals. Even their shapes were shifty: They could appear as crones or as women of surpassing beauty—as they wished.

The most renowned of them were the estranged half sisters of Arthur, daughters of his mother, Igraine, by her first husband. One was Morgause, Queen of Orkney. In his youth, Arthur lay with her all unknowing—perhaps because of a spell she cast, although this is not certain—and fathered a son, Mordred, who was to prove the kingdom's undoing. The other was Morgan le Fay, who in some aspects appeared as a malevolent hag and in some as the most seductive of maidens. It was said that she created an enchanted valley, richly green, watered by a spring that sparkled like diamonds and surrounded by a wall of air. She lured knights into this valley,

With bright banners fluttering from its guardian towers, the castle of Camelot
rose among the spreading forests and fertile fields of England. King Arthur
kept a heroes' court there, in the days when chivalry was in flower.

Lancelot, the finest of Arthur's knights, was hidden in his youth among the fairies of
an underwater kingdom. When he attained the age of knighthood, the fairy Queen—the
Lady of the Lake—ended his enchanted schooling and escorted him to King Arthur.

and they spent their days in pleasure, all thoughts of war forgotten—a living death for a man of chivalry. It was also said that Morgan possessed the power of healing, that she lived on the fairy isle of Avalon with others of her kind and provided a haven for the grievously wounded.

The third in this triad of great enchantresses was known simply as the Lady of the Lake, and she was the most mysterious of all. Some chroniclers wrote that she was a fairy who lived on a crystal mountain beneath the sea, a place where it was always the month of May. Most, however, wrote that her land could be seen under the surface of a certain mountain lake whose name has been lost. It was said that her castle's turrets glimmered like pearls deep within the lake, their pennants waving lightly in the currents, as if in the gentlest of breezes. Or the waters may have been an illusion created by the Lady herself to bar mortal intruders. Treasures—magic rings and cloaks of invisibility—were hidden in her nacreous palaces; Arthur's sword, Excalibur, came from her. It was said that she sometimes imprisoned mortals, but most of her actions—capricious and cloaked in mystery as they were—were beneficent. It was she who protected Lancelot, at once the finest and most tragic of Arthur's heroes, the knight who summed up the greatest joys and sorrows of chivalry.

Lancelot was born in western France, in Benwic, which some say later became Beaune and some Bayonne. He was a King's son, but Ban, his father, was killed in battle when the child Lancelot was no more than a year old. In the confusion of that dangerous time, the Lady of the Lake took the infant away to safety in her kingdom; like the heroes of the ages before him, Lancelot was educated in the other world. And well educated, for the Lady saw not only that he was trained in all the arts of war but also that he understood the obligations and duties of honor. When the time came, and he was ready, she herself presented him to Arthur at Camelot and signified that he should be knighted.

So the young man appeared in Arthur's great hall with the fairy shimmering almost invisible beside him. He was the King's second finely tempered weapon from the Lady of the Lake, a living Excalibur. Tall and strongly made, every inch a king's son, he pledged his life and honor to Arthur and his sword to the King's defense. It was Queen Guinevere who buckled on the sword; the poets wrote that when she had fastened the belt, she raised her eyes to Lancelot with a smile of such blinding sweetness that the young knight's heart contracted with longing. In one instant, he gave all the love of his generous nature forever into Guinevere's keeping.

Young though he was—and shy, for he had not lived much among men— he was well schooled in courtesy. Not a sign escaped him then or for many months. He slipped easily into the camaraderie of Arthur's band of knights; he was openhearted and merry, frank and kind, and his companions grew to love him. And respect him: He had no match among them as a fighter, and this was proved on the jousting field, where he bested them all, more than once.

## A knight caught in enchantment's coils

Reared by one enchantress, Lancelot was captured by another, and she was no less than the mighty Morgan le Fay. It happened one day on his travels, when the knight tethered his horse by a meadow so that he might lie down under an apple tree to sleep.

Four Queens of Faerie with their courtiers rode that way, for Lancelot had unwittingly chosen to rest in their realm. They were the Queen of Northgales, the Queen of Eastland, the Queen of the Out Isles and Morgan le Fay. When they saw the sleeping knight, they reined in and at once fell to quarreling – most unattractively – over who should take him for a lover.

"Let him choose for himself," said Morgan le Fay, to stop the argument. And by a spell, she spirited Lancelot to a prison in her castle.

He awoke hours later to find himself confronted by the four Queens. Morgan was brisk and quite to the point: "You are Lancelot du Lac, King Ban's son," she said. "You love Queen Guinevere, but I assure you, you are lost to her forever. You now may choose one of us for a lover. And you must choose."

"I will not choose. I desire none of you," he said firmly and turned his back. There was a tense silence.

"Then rot in this cell forever," snapped Morgan, and the would-be mistresses swept from the room.

Indeed, Lancelot languished for days in his prison, for binding spells sealed the ways of escape. He required other aid against enchantment.

It came in the form of the lady in waiting who brought him his meals. Lancelot treated her with such courtesy and his chivalry was so renowned that the maiden trusted him. At last one night, she led him from his prison and gave him his freedom.

And as for the lustful Morgan, her failure was but one of several in her pursuit of Lancelot. She tried again to trick him into her arms, but her magic never was a match for the knight's fidelity to his Queen.

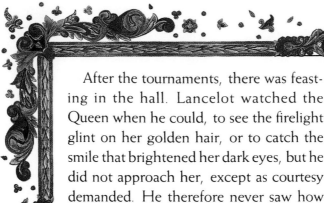

After the tournaments, there was feasting in the hall. Lancelot watched the Queen when he could, to see the firelight glint on her golden hair, or to catch the smile that brightened her dark eyes, but he did not approach her, except as courtesy demanded. He therefore never saw how her eyes rested on him and shone to see his easy grace and gentleness.

Tournaments and feasting wearied young knights after a while, however. When April came, green and showery, they began to leave the fortress, riding past the great gates, through the rye and barley fields that surrounded the castle, into the deep woods that lay beyond. In pairs and singly they left to seek adventure—Gawain and Gaheris, Kay and Bedevere, Bors and Arthur himself. Lancelot, too, rode off to test his courage. He left the gate with a last look at the waiting Queen that told more than he knew.

During the months that followed, tales of Lancelot's deeds drifted back to Camelot, carried by the warriors tiredly returning, by itinerant friars, by wandering bards. They spoke of bloody battles and daring rescues: For the release of two of Arthur's knights, held captive in a castle, Lancelot had fought a sinister lord called Turquin, meeting him in a jousting charge so fierce that both men's horses' backs were broken. While the animals lay dying, the swordplay went on for hours, until Lancelot beheaded Turquin. In Cornwall, it was said, Lancelot killed two giants. And he found Morgan le Fay's enchanted valley with its tribe of languorous prisoners. He slew the knights who guarded the place, including one who was the paramour of the enchantress herself; Lancelot cut off the man's head and presented it to Morgan, thereby freeing her captives.

It was known that the spell on Morgan's valley could be broken only by the valorous; that was the condition of adventure, and victory was the proof of worth. Yet victory was not necessarily victory at arms. Sometimes it was attained by wit or cunning or simply by courage. And in the fragmented tale of Lancelot's adventures—the record of a man going he knew not where and seeking he knew not what, except to prove himself—two incidents served to show his qualities. The truth of where these incidents happened and when has been lost; they simply record two things that befell the knight on his journey. The first adventure was this:

Lancelot came to a wood where the way was lost. His path wound through shadows; tree branches clutched at him. No birds sang, and for a while, he heard nothing but the jingling of his horse's harness bells and the measured fall of its hoofs on the forest floor. At length, however, he caught the sound of music among the leaves—of shawms and lutes and drums. He pressed forward and found himself in a clearing. A tower stood there, and on the flower-dotted grass before it, lords and ladies danced in a ring. They were brightly dressed in the high, pointed headdresses and gaily striped hose of a rich court, but their faces were white and strained and their eyes blank as they danced in compulsive, endless, elegant rotation.

Near them, on the grass, stood a chessboard, and the gold and silver pieces on it moved as gracefully as the dancers, although no hand touched them. Lancelot dismounted and observed for some moments the movement of the chessmen.

A hand touched his wrist gently and he looked down. Beside him stood a dwarf.

his is the rule," said the dwarf. "If a knight plays one side to victory, the prisoners will be released. But only he who is the best knight in the world can win the game." He gave a grating laugh and an awkward bow and disappeared.

Lancelot did not know the captive dancers; he understood only that they were prisoners. His honor demanded that he make the effort to release them, not by a trial at arms but by one of wit. If he lost, he would lose the greatest name a knight could desire—that of the best.

He studied the board with some misgiving. He could play the noble game—as any courtier could—but his skill lay in real warfare, not shadow battles. As he watched, the pieces slid smoothly into gold and silver rows: Behind single ranks of pawns, the rooks, knights, bishops, queens and kings glanced at one another and then stood motionless, waiting for his move.

With a sigh, Lancelot pushed a golden pawn two squares forward into the file: king's pawn to king four. The rank of silver pawns opposite rippled and answered him in kind. The silver king's pawn hopped neatly to its own king four. At Lancelot's back, heedless of the game, the mortal dancers trod their formal pattern.

Lancelot was soon caught up in the ten-

sions of battle and ceased to notice the music or the dancers. He observed the silver queen, looming protectively beside her little king. Her eyes were watchful; her chessmen rotated on their squares—in her direction and back again—before each move was made. She gave no audible orders, but she clearly was the leader of that army, and recognizing his opponent, Lancelot began to enjoy himself. His golden chessmen quivered, restless as blood horses, but they obeyed his movements.

Thrusting into the fray too fast, he lost a pawn to the silver queen. The piece hopped disconsolately to the side. Lancelot paused to consider. The silver queen, he noticed, was a daring but unimaginative leader, spendthrift of her pawn infantry, protective of her knights and careless of her own safety. Lancelot began a flanking action with a bishop and a knight. In five moves, he captured the queen.

She retired from the board with dignity, while the other silver pieces turned on their squares to see her go. But her eyes at the board's edge were watchful as ever.

"You can no longer lead them," said Lancelot to the silver queen. To his astonishment, she winked at him, as if fairly caught, and closed her eyes.

After that, his task was easy, for the action of the silver pieces grew progressively more confused. Pawns clustered anxiously at the center of the fray. A rook moved out of turn—and on the diagonal, as if it were a bishop—before it caught itself and retreated in disorder. The knights tried to advance together and collided. They picked themselves up and returned to position.

It was over some minutes later. "Check,"

said Lancelot, moving a golden pawn. His own queen glared proudly down the file at the silver king.

There was a pause while the silver pieces surveyed their hopeless position. No move could save the silver king for long.

"Yield, recreants," said Sir Lancelot, grinning. With a metallic click, the silver king toppled over.

Lancelot straightened himself. There was silence in the little clearing. The music had stopped, and the dancers, too, had

## The lily maid of Astolat

Many a maiden adored Sir Lancelot, but his heart had been pledged to Queen Guinevere from the moment he joined King Arthur's company at Camelot. So the maidens sighed in vain; most gave up the chase. Only one ever matched with her affection the perfect, tragic exclusivity of Lancelot's passion for the Queen.

That woman was Elaine of Astolat, the fair, the lovable, the lily maid. When she first saw Lancelot, from the tower of her father's castle, she did not even know who he was. He was riding in disguise to test his valor without the support of his formidable reputation. Elaine's father gave him shelter for the night, as was the custom in those courteous days; Elaine sat by him in her father's hall. And when she found that he intended to fight in a tourney held each year at Camelot, she asked whether he would wear her favor.

This was an expected courtesy, for knights often rode into battle wearing ribbons or silks from the ladies they loved. Lancelot never did: He could not wear Guinevere's favor and he would wear no other. He refused Elaine's request, but when he saw her stricken look, he relented. A favor, after all, would add to his disguise. But Elaine took the gesture seriously.

So Lancelot rode onto the jousting field bearing a white shield and wearing Elaine's scarlet sleeve, embroidered with pearls. He was not recognized. He unseated forty knights that day and was himself wounded by a spear. He rode back to Elaine with his injury. She nursed him lovingly for months, and when he was hail again, she asked to marry him.

He told her, as gently as he could, that he would never marry. She offered to become his paramour.

Appalled, Lancelot said that his heart was given elsewhere and returned alone to Camelot.

And Elaine simply wasted and died for love. Her deathbed, at her request, was a barge set in a river to drift to Camelot. It was Lancelot who found her and he who sadly buried her.

stopped. Color returned to their faces and intelligence to their eyes. They bowed to Lancelot where he stood, the best knight in the world, and faded back among the trees, returning freely to whatever land had sheltered them before they had been

entrapped. Lancelot turned and mounted and set off once more.

The next adventure, or the next, or the next — the chronology was often unclear — was this: Lancelot came to a gate by the road and found a maiden. He saluted her, and she, weeping, told him her tale. She begged his aid for her brother's sake: The young man had slain a knight called Gilbert in fair combat and had been wounded himself. Now Sir Gilbert lay dead in a chapel beyond the gate, but his widow had placed a curse on the victor: The young man's injuries would not heal unless a knight was brave enough to take Sir Gilbert's sword and touch the wounds with it and cut a strip of the dead man's clothing and bind the wounds with it.

Lancelot smiled at the maiden. He dismounted, leaving his horse by the gate, and strode to the chapel.

The small stone building stood alone among the trees. The task seemed easy enough, until Lancelot saw what guarded the building. Thirty knights in black armor stood leaning on their spears beside the chapel wall. They were motionless. Their heads turned, however, toward the sound of Lancelot's footsteps, and with a frightening mechanical gait they began to walk toward him, eyes glinting red and teeth glittering white in mouths that stretched in insane, blank smiles. A fearful sweet stench surrounded them.

Sweat prickled on Lancelot's neck and ugly fear coiled in his belly. He put up his shield and walked toward the chapel door, while the silent creatures crowded close. Shouldering them aside, he entered. He found the corpse and pulled its sword from the scabbard and a strip of silk from its tunic, and as he did so, the ground beneath him trembled.

He turned. The silent knights stood at his back, a mass of darkness blocking the chapel door. The dead man's sword in hand, he set his jaw and walked directly toward them. And when he was close, they shuffled aside to let him pass. They spoke then, in toneless chorus.

"Put down that sword, Sir Lancelot. Leave it, or you will die."

But Lancelot stood now in the light of the sun, safe outside the perilous cha-

moistened her red lips with a sharp little tongue, and her green eyes shone at him. "Come to me now, and kiss me."

But Lancelot's heart was given to Guinevere. He shook his head once more.

When he did so, the woman seemed to fade; her image wavered in the air. "I have loved you long," she told him. "I know where your heart tends. But I could have had your body by me, had your heart stopped its beating. I could enjoy you dead as well as alive." She was the sorceress Hellawes, one of Morgan le Fay's kind, a death-bringer and a lover of death. Lance-

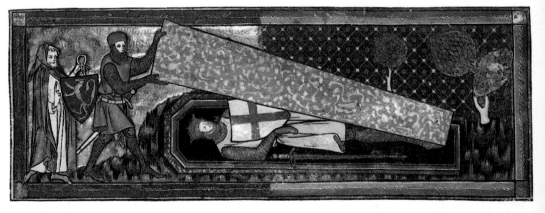

pel. He shook his head and then he stared.

A young woman, black-haired, green-eyed, red-lipped and smiling, stood in the yard. She wore the weeds of a widow.

"Lancelot, put down the sword," she said softly. "If you take it, you will not leave this place alive."

"I will not do it," he replied.

She clasped her hands to her breast then and gave a smile of great relief.

"Had you done as I asked, then truly you would have died," she said.

"Then I should have been a fool to obey you," responded the knight.

"True enough, my chevalier." She

lot's courage and his steadfast heart defeated her, and it is said that she died soon after he left to heal the young knight's wounds with her own husband's sword.

Such were the tales told in King Arthur's hall. For in the autumn, when the days grew short and the evenings chill, those knights who survived their testing in the wilderness came back to Camelot one by one, lean and brown, battered and weary. On long winter nights, when the fires blazed bright and the snow blew outside, they rested and told tales of adventures, and the man they named most often was Lancelot, the flower of them all.

*The valiant knew death awaited and they faced it with calm: On a journey once, Lancelot found his own tomb, marked with his name, but still went on to seek adventure.*

He was the King's champion—and the Queen's. He offered his fealty to Guinevere, and all knew he was the Queen's knight. This was, of course, an established custom in a chivalric court, with its formal patterns of devotion and its elaborate courtesies. Great ladies always had chevaliers, whose attitude was that of selfless and unrequited love and whose reward was no more than a smile from the beloved. The King viewed the proceedings with kindly amusement: Lancelot was as a son to Arthur, and the champion's honoring of the Queen honored the King as well.

Queen. The tale of the abduction was a convoluted one, but the main events were these: A Prince named Meleagant, who in various battles had taken a number of Arthur's knights hostage, demanded the Queen in place of them because he had a passion for her. Guinevere bravely journeyed to his country, the kingdom of Gorre. It was commonly said of the place that no one who went there ever returned.

In any event, Lancelot set out after the Queen, riding hard until he came to the borderlands. There he fought several knights—outriders, possibly, of Melea-

But Lancelot's love for the Queen was no ritual expression of courtly behavior. When only at the beginning of manhood, he had given her his whole heart, and his was a steadfast nature. He showed his fidelity for all to see. There were no half-secret dalliances with serving maids or ladies of the court, as might have been expected from so vigorous a young man.

And a time arrived when Guinevere answered Lancelot's affection and became his mistress, although both knew the affair was a betrayal of the King and a stain on Lancelot's bright honor.

It happened after the abduction of the

gant. Little is known of the battle, since all that was found were dead horses, lying on the ground, their bright caparisons dark with blood. Lancelot's was among them.

He himself was not there. He had pressed on toward Gorre in pursuit of Guinevere. But he traveled in an odd and unbecoming way. An armed and armored knight, already fatigued from battle, was an awkward man, in no position to walk far. Lancelot found himself near one of the hamlets typical of the borderlands—a cluster of thatched houses where scrawny hens scratched in unyielding dirt and listless children stared at him blankly. There were

*Lancelot once broke a spell and freed the prisoners it bound by winning*
*at chess against a magical opponent. Some said that he then*
*took the enchanted chessboard to Queen Guinevere as a battle trophy.*

several mules, but a mule is a small beast and lacks the strength to carry a knight.

In the dirt track that formed the village street, however, stood a wooden cart, harnessed to a nag and driven by a dwarf. The driver looked at Lancelot with the sliding, sideways glance of his kind, smirked and said, "Get in, knight. I will take you to Gorre, where you will find your Queen."

Lancelot hesitated. Carts were for criminals bound for the stocks or the headsman's block. Misshapen outcasts like dwarfs drove them; only the vilest ever

The river was black and swift; the trees overhanging its banks were bare and dead.

"Bridge," said the dwarf with a jerk of his head and an ugly, derisive grimace.

There was a bridge, a single gleaming span wedged between tree trunks on either side of the water. It was a gigantic sword, narrow as a ribbon, cutting edge up. On the far bank, among the trees, was a squat tower—the prison that held the Queen.

On hands and knees, Lancelot crossed the sword bridge. His legs were protected by his greaves, but his palms split open

rode in them. Lancelot was a proud young man and he did not care to look like a fool. But he had no choice, it seemed. He climbed into the cart. The dwarf flicked his whip, and the unlikely conveyance set off. The children crowed and jeered.

They traveled for a day, through hamlets as mean as the first, where poor creatures came running to jeer and point at the knight hunched uncomfortably in the creaking cart. At each new settlement, the inhabitants gathered in the road, to howl with laughter at the sight.

At last, however, the cart halted at the verge of a river. "Here," said the dwarf briefly. Lancelot climbed out of the cart.

with his weight on the blade, and blood dripped down into the water below. Stolidly, he crawled into the land of Gorre.

Meleagant was waiting for him; so was the Queen in the tower. The rules of chivalry held: While Guinevere watched, her champion battled her captor and brought Meleagant to his knees. He was forced to guarantee Guinevere's safety while she remained in Gorre and to give her into the care of Lancelot for the journey home.

But when Lancelot went to the Queen afterward, she turned away imperiously. It was said that—still pursuing the courtly nonsense of the time—she was angered because she had heard of his hesitation in

*To save Queen Guinevere—hostage of an evil Prince—Sir Lancelot cast aside his knightly dignity: Unhorsed in battle, he followed after her with the only means he found at hand, a criminal's cart.*

mounting the dwarf's cart; he had put his pride before her safety. At any rate, they quarreled, and those nearby saw Lancelot stride grimly off, into the forests of Gorre.

Word soon came to Guinevere that Lancelot had been slain, and then Guinevere knew her heart indeed. When he returned to her tower to take her home, she summoned him in secret to her chamber, and from that time on, they were lovers.

The adventure had a happy ending: Lancelot returned the Queen to the King at Camelot in safety. But it was a sad be-

Arthur's court had deteriorated with the years; it was becoming a place of faction and intrigue. The source of much of this was Mordred, Arthur's son by his sister Morgause. Mordred was a secret, smiling villain nurtured by hatred. When the young Arthur discovered that he had lain with his sister and what the issue was — Mordred, born on May Day — he had had all infants born on that day in Britain gathered together and put into a boat, to be brought to him, for what end none could tell. The boat had foundered; only the in-

ginning, for the Queen and her champion could not bear to be long apart. They were discreet, but the change showed. In place of veneration on the one side and gracious acknowledgment on the other, Lancelot and Guinevere showed the signs common among illicit lovers: secret smiles and whispered conversations, sudden angers and jealousies — quickly over — hands that brushed together as if by accident, eyes that held a glance too long. The King seemed oblivious, but the courtiers saw, and some of them bided their time, knowing that the information would be useful.

The splendid closeness and honor of

fant Mordred, washed ashore while still alive, had survived. Mordred thought — perhaps rightly — that his father had sought to kill him. And though Arthur had no legitimate children, Mordred's bastardy barred him from the throne. At court, Mordred served his father with apparent devotion, and sowed the seeds of dissension where he could. He gathered around him a group of young, dissatisfied knights, and he watched Lancelot and Guinevere avidly. When he became sure of what he suspected, Mordred would act and the end would be the destruction of Camelot and all it had embodied.

*To enter the land of Gorre, where his Queen was held prisoner,*
*Lancelot had to cross a bridge that was a sword. He made the crossing*
*balancing with his hands, at the cost of fearsome wounds.*

# Sir Percival

The heroes of the Round Table were knights errant who roamed the world in search of adventure. And their world offered wonders: Sir Percival de Gales once came upon the castle of an enchantress. There, he found a fellow knight chained to a pillar outside, and unhesitatingly, with a deft stroke of his sword, Percival severed the chains and freed the warrior. When he heard the knight's tale he went after the enchantress herself: She bound men by spells just for the pleasure of it. Percival was proof against her charms, however, and when he had her at his mercy, he commanded her to release her prisoners. And one by one, all around the castle, scattered stones and boulders moved. Each stone took human shape and spoke. Each one had contained a mortal captured by the enchantress.

# Sir Bors

This is the tale of Sir Bors, who by magic was dissuaded from fratricide, so that he might be pure and worthy of great quests to come. One day, Bors came to a crossroads and saw two desperate sights—his brother Lionel held captive by strange warriors, and not far distant, a maiden in the hands of brigands. Bors left his brother to his fate and raced to succor the maiden. When he returned he found Lionel free and blind with rage at the choice. The brothers fought savagely then, and Bors had the advantage, for he was the stronger. But when he moved to slay Lionel and finish the quarrel, bright fire erupted from his shield and formed a wall of flame. In the face of this miracle, Bors lowered his sword and allowed his brother to live. But he had no more to do with Lionel.

# Sir Gareth

The enemies knights encountered had curious powers: Sir Gareth of Orkney searched long months for a worthy foe. Guided by a maid, he found that foe in a fortress in a forest. From its trees swung the bodies of forty knights—failed challengers of the lord of the fortress. Near the bodies hung an ivory horn. From a tower of the castle the fairest of maidens regarded Gareth plaintively through iron bars; she was the imprisoned sister of his guide. Gareth blew the ivory horn and the defender of the fortress burst through its gates to battle Gareth. Like the sun, he grew in strength from dawn until noon, when he fought like seven men at once. But after noon, his strength waned, and good Gareth defeated him in bloody battle. Gareth freed the maiden, and took her for his own.

# Sir Gawain

An adventure that ended in great sadness for Sir Gawain began at King Arthur's wedding feast, when an enchanted white hart bounded into the King's hall. Tormented by court hounds, the small deer fled, and at Merlin's bidding, Sir Gawain gave chase.

He pursued the deer to a distant castle and in his excitement he let his hounds kill it. But the deer belonged to a knight called Blamoure, and this knight killed the dogs for revenge. Then, raging, Gawain battled him and brought him to his knees. Blamoure cried mercy, but Gawain raised his sword for the kill—and slew an innocent. Blamoure's lady took the death blow. Gawain carried the shame in his heart for the rest of his life: Ignoring a cry for mercy, he had done murder.

# Chapter Four

# The Noblest Quest of All

When Arthur ruled over all Britain, one remote tract of the island differed from all the rest. Far north of the fields and forests that enfolded Camelot, an ominous change settled upon the landscape. The green canopies of oak and beech, the carpets of bluebell and veined anemone disappeared; instead of meadows where dog rose clambered over hedgerows and clumps of golden kingcup shone in stream beds, instead of the birds' chatter and the browsing of deer, there was stark desolation. Sand flats, rock heaps, stone and rubble sprawled over a waterless plain rimmed by bleak gray mountains.

A man might walk for days over the blasted ground and see no evidence of life, save for a vulture perched on the blackened limb of a leafless tree. There were habitations, it is true, but these were thinly spread over the arid expanses, and they presented a hard, gaunt aspect at one with the scenery around them. This region was called the Waste Land.

In a broad brown valley there, a granite island rose from a parched lake bed. At the island's center stood a stone slab on which was incised, in letters now partly erased by the blowing dust, this epitaph: *Here lieth Balin le Savage that was the knight with two swords, and he that smote the Dolorous Stroke.*

A cairn of pebbles rose behind the stone, and over the tableau, silently preserving its secrets, reared the decayed fortifications of a castle.

The bones that were sheltered in the tomb were those of one of Arthur's knights, who decades before had been sent into exile. A skilled and fearless warrior from the wilds of Northumberland, Balin was aptly named the Savage. He had an insane temper, and when the fury was upon him, he was murderous. He had once been imprisoned for killing a cousin of the King's. Shortly after his release he killed a sorceress who had uttered threats against him, and it was for this act that he was sent away.

He left doubly cursed. The sword he carried was not the one he had been given when he was knighted. It was one that he had taken from a fairy woman, and she had laid a fate upon it. Her sword, she said, would slay the man Balin loved best. And the fairy's weapon bore a second, even harsher sentence. The enchanter Merlin had seen something in the steel, and when Balin left the court, Merlin made the young knight a prophecy.

"The man who bears that sword will

strike the Dolorous Stroke, though not with the sword itself," said the wizard gravely. "He will bring drought and famine to the earth."

**B**ut Balin, mounted and eager to put his shame behind him, shrugged impatiently and spurred his horse and left the gates of Arthur's fortress, riding alone into the world. He bore a shield with no device, for he did not care to be recognized. He did not look behind him.

For some months Balin traveled with his brother Balan, who came loyally from Northumberland to meet him. The pair had fine, free action before Balan left on adventures of his own. The enemies they defeated—petty, overweening kings who sought to disrupt Arthur's peace, tyrannical barons who kept ugly court in secret mountain fastnesses—trickled into Camelot to pledge fealty to King Arthur, and Balin's star began to rise again.

Balin, however, was driven by forces he could not fathom. Not by guilt: It was unlikely that such a man would feel remorse for a murder he had done in thoughtless rage. Not by fear—although from time to time the fairy's curse and the wizard's prophecy crossed his mind. His restless wandering went on; he was much alone in the northern reaches.

It happened one bright summer day that he fell in with a knight called Herlews le Berbeus, who rode with a young woman, intent on some business of his lord's. The three rode along companionably for some miles, chatting of this and that in the way of travelers. Then Balin heard a high whistling; before he could turn in the saddle, a spear hurtled through the air and, with an awful thud, pierced the breast of Sir Herlews. The knight's horse shied. Herlews clutched his chest, and blood spilled out over his fingers.

"Garlon has killed me," Herlews said. "You will not find him here. He has the gift of invisibility. Follow my lady to him." And he died.

They left him in the meadow, stretched out in seemly fashion with his sword in his hands. Urged by the weeping woman, Balin rode on, swearing vengeance in his fellow knight's name.

They came to a forest and in it overtook a solitary knight, whose name was Perin de Mountbeliard. As they paused to speak, however, death came again. Without a warning hoofbeat or a rustle of crushed leaves, a spear flew through the air. Sir Perin fell, and the last word on his lips was Garlon's name. Frustrated, Balin searched about him for an enemy who was not there. A blush of rage—which would have been familiar to his companions in Arthur's court—darkened Balin's face. His hands began to tremble. But the lady only pressed him on, to a watchtower that rose near the forest track.

The men there sheltered the travelers and told them the tale. Balin was at the border of the country of King Pellam, a good King whose lands prospered with his goodness. In Pellam's court, however, was a shadow—the King's brother Garlon, who roamed the borderlands, invisible at will, slaying at random and for pleasure. It was the way of a coward, the action of a murderer.

In the morning Balin set off for King Pellam's land.

The road to Castle Carbonek, Pellam's seat, rose steeply between two rounded mountains. From the crest of the pass could be seen a broad green valley, hemmed by steep hills and quartered by orchards and well-tended fields. Straight ahead, rising sharply into the air, stood a vertical bulwark of rock half a mile wide. At its summit, reflected in the lake that surrounded the rock, rose a castle, a rambling edifice of ramparts and towers, surmounted by the fluttering standards of Pellam of Listinoise.

The pair rode through the fields and orchards to the bridge that spanned the encircling water. Balin and the lady were taken to the King.

In the hall they found a company of courtiers, colorful as wild flowers on a summer's day. Troubadours were there, and jesters, and servants bearing flagons. Among them stood King Pellam, a tall and kindly man, who welcomed Balin and the lady and offered them the shelter of his roof. Balin made his bow, left the lady with the King and walked slowly around the hall.

"Who is Garlon?" he asked a serving man. The servant pointed to a figure near the hearth, a heavy-set man with trim black hair and beard, who stood at his ease surveying the company. Balin stared fixedly at him. Alerted, perhaps, by the intensity of the gaze, Garlon sauntered toward the stranger.

"Find a seat, bumpkin, and cease your staring," he said.

And Balin's rage came full upon him then. Howling the names of Herlews and Perin, Balin drew his enchanted sword and swung it in a vicious arc. The gleaming blade bit through Garlon's skull and cleft down to his shoulders. The hideous form slumped gushing and twitching onto the flagstones of the floor. What expression could be discerned on the two halves of the face was one of surprise.

A moment no longer than a heartbeat passed. Then the courtiers shouted and rushed toward the strange knight. King Pellam was at the fore, his sword flashing to strike. But Balin parried the blow with his own dripping weapon, though the force of the assault sent the sword spinning from his hand into the pool of blood forming at his feet.

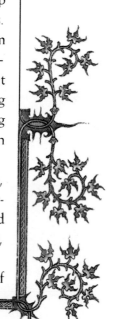

**W**eaponless, Balin fled through the archway of the hall into the corridors of the unfamiliar castle, searching for a means of defense—or escape. At once, he found himself in a labyrinth of twisting, torchlit passages. Balin ran up curving stairs and through dim corridors. The shouts of his pursuers echoed from the stones: He knew not where they were—or where he was. He came to a wall set with deep windows. He ran swiftly along the wall, and saw in flashes the changing prospects of blue sky and heavy-laden trees that lay outside.

At the end of the wall was a low arch, framing the first steps of a circular staircase. He had reached a tower. He ducked through the archway and ran up the stair, spiraling dizzily as he followed its coils.

At the top of the stair was a door of

apple wood, graven with strange images Balin did not recognize. He paused. Save for his heavy breathing, all was silent. He heard no following footsteps, no clang of swords, no angry shouts. A profound and darkling silence settled around him, a thick and peaceful blanket of shadow. Gone to ground, he thought. He pushed the door silently open to reveal the room it guarded.

The chamber was not large. Its walls were hung with black velvet embroidered in gold; its floor was a mosaic of shimmering stones. The ceiling was vaulted and painted a blue as deep as that of the evening sky; stars of gold winked among its arches. In the center of this grandeur stood a table that bore an object Balin could not see, for the object was covered with a cloth whose white folds marked its shape. Balin blinked. Hovering over the object, floating freely in the air, was a glowing spear, point down. Around the object, light shifted and trembled, as if silent harmonies played there, or as if some mighty magic breathed.

Balin shied; this was a place of old, old gods. Immense and unknown powers were sleeping here: It was as if the starry, shining chamber were a sacred vessel that held the beating heart of the living world. The room was no place for mere mortals.

A footstep sounded loud on the stair and Balin whirled around. Outlined in the doorway, just outside the radiance of the room, stood a still, tall figure. It was King Pellam, who sheathed his sword and waited, motionless, regarding Balin the transgressor.

Trapped, the knight moved with the speed of a beast. He reached his hand into the shimmering light and seized the spear from the air and struck at the King's groin.

He had an instant — only an instant — to know what he had done. He felt a scorching pain across his palm, where the spear had burned him; he heard a rumble and the howl of the wind; he saw in jittering flashes visions of a head bathed in blood, of a spear splitting flesh. And last, Balin saw the crumpling figure of the King, where it wavered in the light. Then the darkness closed around him.

He awakened slowly, to feel pebbles crushed against his cheek and dirt in his dry mouth. He noticed without emotion that he was cold. He opened his eyes and stared up at a gray sky.

Balin moved his eyes painfully and saw towering rubbles of stone and scorched wood. Someone sat beside him: Merlin the Enchanter. The old man was silent, staring at the shattered landscape. Balin did not ask how Merlin had found him: The ways of the wizard passed all understanding.

"You have entered the web of your fate now, Balin," said the Enchanter. "Unthinking as an animal you took the cursed fairy sword; blindly you followed where anger led. You transgressed on the sacred elder powers when you invaded the sanctuary of the Grail. The King lies maimed in his broken house. And his land will suffer with him: No water flows here now, no plant will grow, no bird will sing. Only a word will deliver the King, and you do not have the word."

"What must I do?" asked Balin dully.

*The Quest for the Grail came about because of the Dolorous Stroke: A hot-blooded knight called Balin maimed the King of Listinoise with a sacred spear. By its power, Listinoise became a wasteland that could be delivered only by the best knight in the world.*

"What you must," Merlin answered. "Here is the sword; follow where it leads until you come to the end."

So Balin rose obediently and buckled on the fairy sword that had been struck from him by King Pellam. Balin found a horse to carry him and rode out wearily to meet his fate. As he left Castle Carbonek, he turned and raised a hand to bid Merlin farewell. But the wizard had vanished.

The countryside around seemed to alter as Balin passed. A cold wind blew steadily at his back. In the orchards, blackened fruit covered the ground; yellow leaves blew past him and rattled on the road. In the fields, the wheat stood unharvested, and when he came close, he saw that the stalks were sere and brown. Sometimes he saw dead rabbits and deer by the path, their skin already rippling with the feeding of maggots beneath. Sometimes he passed farmhouses whose shutters flapped unattended in the wind.

After a while, Balin ceased to look around; he kept his eyes on the road. He was therefore startled when a loud voice hailed him. An old man stepped from the scrub and angrily ordered him back. But behind the old man were heart-lifting green trees and behind the trees, white towers. He had come to the border of Pellam's domain, it seemed. Would he be allowed to pass out of the kingdom?

He spurred the horse past the old man and into the sun-dappled wood. In the distance a hunter's horn blew the kill, and Balin thought briefly of his boyhood hunts in the forests of Northumberland.

Beyond the wood, hard by a shining river, stood a castle, ablaze with banners. On its ramparts people smiled and beckoned. A lady called down to him. "Join us when you have jousted for us," she said merrily. "Our champion is the Knight of the River."

It seemed a curious greeting indeed for a man so obviously weary, but Balin donned his helmet, put up his blackened shield and rode in the direction that the lady had indicated.

Balin found a field and on it his adversary, as anonymous behind the knight's visor as he himself was. They saluted briefly and set to battle.

They followed the ritual of the tourney in a businesslike way: first the jousting with lances, then the swordplay. They were evenly matched; Balin found the turn of thrust and parry was a pleasure. Then his adversary dealt him a searing stroke to the shoulder. With the pain came Balin's old rage. He pressed forward fiercely, the sword of Faerie leaping in his hand—and was fiercely met.

The battle went on for hours, but at last the stranger's sword entered Balin's throat. Balin replied with a vicious thrust upward into the man's breast. Then Balin fell, his lifeblood bubbling in his mouth. He pulled his helmet off and spat; the stranger knight lay near him, his hauberk split, his blood pulsing out. The man's helmet concealed his face.

"Brave knight, let me know your name. I have never met my match before." Balin said, and waited, fighting death off for the answer that must come.

"I am Balan of Northumberland. I am brother to King Arthur's knight Balin le Savage."

The strife was over, the pattern complete. Balin had killed the man he loved best in the world. It was said that Merlin appeared then. He took the sword of Faerie and embedded it to the hilt in a block of red marble and hid it by enchantment. Merlin had the brothers buried together, under the stone that told Balin's tale in

lapidary letters: Balin had struck the Dolorous Stroke that violated the power of the Grail and injured King Pellam, and brought waste to Pellam's land.

As the tomb was made, the leaves around the castle withered and fell; the grass browned; the river sank to mud and then to cracked earth. The people disappeared as the Waste Land embraced their kingdom, and soon cold winds whined through their empty, crumbling halls.

Thus, according to the chroniclers, began the greatest venture of the company of the Round Table, the last before the shadows closed around that valiant brotherhood. Word came drifting back to Camelot – brought perhaps by Merlin and perhaps by wayfarers – that somewhere in Britain was an ancient kingdom, laid waste because its King had been wounded. This was not unusual then: In many old countries, ruler and land were bound in profound union, so that the fertility of the land depended on the vigor of the King. But the death of the country had a second cause: Its blight came about because the magical object that rested at its heart had been desecrated.

And therein lay the mystery that has baffled the inquisitive from that day to this. What was the Grail? Whence came its mystic power?

The Grail was a never-ending source of abundance, and the lance that hovered over it was a weapon of immeasurable strength. Such objects had been sung about since humans had words to sing. As far away as India, sages told of fire that had been stolen from the sun, and of a spear that brought fertility even to sun-baked earth. In Classical Greece, it was said that a divine cup held all the elements of life; the cup was the font of newborn souls. In Ireland there were tales of the treasures of the Tuatha Dé Danaan, a race of warriors that had invaded the island before the time of humankind, bringing a caldron that eternally provided food, and a spear that no enemy could survive.

Legends abounded. All of them linked the Grail with fertility and sustenance and safety. None agreed in other regards, not even as to what the Grail was. Some said a cup, some a caldron, some a dish, some a stone, some an emerald that had fallen from heaven. Some said it appeared in different forms at different times.

The Christians, as their religion spread, gave the Grail their own definition. They said that the spear Balin had seized was the very same spear that had pierced Christ's side when he was crucified on the Cross; the Grail, they claimed, was a golden chalice that had been used to catch his blood. Both relics had been carried to Britain by a soldier named Joseph of Arimathea, who built a castle to shelter the talismans and passed the duty of guarding them down through the generations of his family to King Pellam.

At the center, however, the matter of the Grail remained a mystery far more ancient than Christianity. All that was really known in King Arthur's time was this: Somewhere in Britain a land lay under a wasting enchantment, its King wounded and the talisman that shielded the kingdom damaged in some way. It was said that

Escorted by an aged hermit, a young knight clothed in crimson appeared at
King Arthur's court to join the company of the Round Table. He was the son of Sir
Lancelot and of the Grail Maiden. He was invincible. His name was Galahad.

only the best knight in the world could restore the fertility of the land and the health of the King; and it was said that the deed would be accomplished with words, not with weapons, although the words were not known. One thing more became clear: The valiant knight would be a man of Pellam's own blood.

But all the rest was remarkably elusive. Even the Waste Land and Castle Carbonek appeared and disappeared in baffling fashion for decades after Balin's venture. Knights might ride through the district and see nothing but earth and stone. Or they might see King Pellam's palace rising from the ruins, where a moment before no palace had been. And those who entered the castle's gates told later of mysterious adventure.

Lancelot, the most valiant knight in the world, came upon the castle in the course of a different quest. In the midst of desolation, he found grandeur. He was admitted to the ruined castle and taken to the hall. It shone with splendor: Torches flickered gold on the walls, jewels glinted in the hair of the court ladies, the fire leaped red in the hearth. On the King's dais lay the pallet that bore the wounded King. He greeted Lancelot courteously and spoke with him gently, and all the while he watched the knight with aged, compassionate eyes.

Then, with a wave of his hand, the King showed wonders: At his sign, music rose in the hall, although no musicians could be seen. A procession entered—maidens bearing steaming goblets, pages carrying platters heaped with gleaming fruit. Among them was a youth who bore a golden spear. From its tip, a rivulet of scarlet trickled. With the youth was a maiden of surpassing beauty, and in her long white hands she carried an object. Light quivered around her, brighter than the sun, but whatever it was she carried was hidden by a coverlet of white cloth. Lancelot longed to see the object, but this was to be denied him.

It was a deep and moving magic, although Lancelot could not tell what mystery moved him. Tears welled in his eyes, and he turned to the King. But Pellam said only, "She who bears the Grail is my daughter." He signaled again. The procession left the hall. The shimmering light faded, and the music died.

But one thing more happened. Lancelot stayed in the castle that night and fathered a son on Pellam's daughter. It was brought about by magic: Lancelot, having given his heart and his honor to Arthur's Queen, desired no other woman. During the night, a serving maid came to him with a ring of Guinevere's and a summons, and so bemused was he by enchantment that he believed the Queen to be nearby. Lancelot went without question to the tryst. When he awoke in sunshine, however, he awoke beside the Grail Maiden, King Pellam's daughter. The ring had disappeared. Angered at the trickery and grief-stricken by the act, Lancelot left the castle.

The result of this union made his appearance years later at a time near midsummer, when flowers nodded in the gardens of Camelot and nightingales sang

*When the time was right, the Grail itself appeared for a brief moment at Camelot, swathed in mystery. Inspired by its fleeting magic, the knights of the Round Table set off on the Quest to find its true resting place. Their ladies armed them and wept to see them go.*

all the night through. An aged man requested an audience with King Arthur and was admitted. The old man entered, a bent figure clothed in white wool. A youth – hardly more than a boy – entered with him. The youth's face was that of Lancelot, but it lacked the warmth of the champion's: The blue eyes were cool, the mouth was set in an expressionless line. Merlin moved to stand beside King Arthur. Lancelot gazed upon his son, and then he turned his head away.

"This is Galahad," said the old man, and bowing, he withdrew from the hall.

The company stirred; there were covert glances at Lancelot. Only Merlin the Enchanter spoke.

"We will have the tests," he said calmly.

**m**erlin led the youth to the place at the Round Table called the Siege Perilous, where no one but the best knight in the world might sit, on pain of death by magic. Lancelot, called the best of knights, had always refused the seat: He knew that his love for Queen Guinevere was a stain on his honor, no matter how bright his valor might shine. Without hesitation, Lancelot's son took the place, and all saw the letters that sprang like flames from the wood: *This is the Siege of Sir Galahad, the Haut Prince.*

"Follow me," said the Enchanter, and led the company out of the hall to the river that sparkled below the ramparts of the fortress. In the silence Merlin spoke, and no one recognized the words he used. On the riverbank a stone of red marble appeared, and embedded in the stone was a mighty sword. On its jeweled hilt, in shining letters, were engraved these words:

*Never shall man take me hence, but only he by whose side I ought to hang, and he shall be the best knight in the world.*

Merlin turned to Lancelot, but the great knight shook his head. It was Galahad who stepped calmly forward and easily drew the sword from the stone. "That is Balin's sword," said Merlin. "It seeks redemption."

So the company returned to the fortress, with Galahad among them. They tested him, of course, in the days that followed. Fighting was their genius. They tested him in the jousting lists and on the field, and with negligent ease he felled them all, as his father once had before him. Only Lancelot refrained from trying the skill of Galahad. In their love and courtesy his companions of the Round Table made no comment on this.

To Galahad, too, the knights had little to say. He was an admirable fighter, fierce and skilled, but he was not one with them. He kept himself distant from men, and he had no interest in women. He was never seen to laugh.

The chroniclers of later years made Galahad into a creature of remorseless and unappealing purity, a plaster saint bathed in a sea of sanctity, but the picture seems askew. He was conceived with the aid of old magic – whether that magic was King Pellam's or another's is not known – and was born for only one purpose: to restore life to the Waste Land. In his veins flowed the blood of the best knight in the world. He was Lancelot without the stain. In his veins also flowed the blood of the daughter of the Grail King, and in those

*After the last farewells were said, King Arthur's knights rode out, hearts high, and thus the company of the Round Table began to disband as each man pursued his private quest.*

*Accompanied by bands of angels, young Sir Galahad journeyed through
dark forests and across deep seas to find the Waste Land and the Grail. And
triumph attended his adventures, for Galahad was the best knight in the world.*

days, the matter of blood was paramount.

Galahad had been trained for his purpose all his life by wise men at Castle Carbonek. Now he was ready to fulfill his purpose and fulfill it in the manner of heroes. Before the eyes of the valiant, he had to prove his valor. Cold and humorless, he sharpened his skill and waited for the signal that would send him on his way.

It came one evening, toward the end of summer, when the companions of the Round Table were feasting in Arthur's hall. Amid the laughter and the singing only Galahad was silent—but that was not unusual. He kept himself a little apart from the others and watched a dusky beam of late sunlight that streamed through a narrow window, gilding the flagstones

wilderness to prove themselves. Only Galahad appeared unchanged, but he was a very young man.

The knights fell silent. And in the air above them, trembling just out of reach, the Grail appeared, draped in white and floating of its own accord.

In a moment, the talisman was gone, but the air seemed incandescent still. And words echoed in the memories of the men:

"He who would deliver the Waste Land must journey through peril to find the Grail Castle and ask the question. He who asks will find an answer and he will be the best knight in the world."

And the following day at dawn, the last quest began. King Arthur watched pensively as his knights – the pride of his youth and the flowering of his earliest dreams – clattered out of the gate of his fortress, their armor bright, their horses gleaming. Guinevere wept.

The best left first: Gawain and Bors, Ector and Lionel and Lancelot. And Galahad. And Percival.

Percival was of particular interest, for in his veins as well as in Galahad's flowed the blood of Pellam, the Grail King, and Percival was one of the few on the Quest who would see the Grail itself, for only the finest of men ever got a glimpse of the mystic object.

Percival, alas, was something of a fool. He became a mature and accomplished knight, but he was always a young boy in essence, a creature of wide-eyed, honest gullibility who never disbelieved another's word, who obeyed everyone's advice and who never understood the meaning of doubt or reflection.

and making rainbows from the jewels that the knights wore on their belts.

The light grew stronger. It bathed the faces of Arthur's companions, so that the deep creases in the flesh that betrayed their weary years – and their growing, secret animosities – seemed to vanish. They looked like the young men they once had been, youths who had set out into the

He was Pellam's nephew, brought up by his mother in a forest, completely innocent of any knowledge of chivalry – or indeed, of civilization. When he first encountered deer in the forest, he thought they were goats that had lost their horns. Percival chased the animals for miles, caught them and penned them in his mother's yard. His mother sighed for his wits and marveled at his fleetness. He gaped at the first knights he saw riding through the forest, thought they must be gods and, to their intense irritation, fell on his knees to worship them.

When he learned their real vocation, he decided without hesitation to strive for knighthood. He left his mother weeping and set off with a short spear, a ridiculously ragged coat and a list of maternal rules, which he always obeyed. He was a literal, likable fellow to the tips of his toes.

He arrived at Camelot and within a day fought his first man, a villainous knight who had entered the fortress for purposes of theft and fled with a golden goblet. Percival killed him with the small spear. Some moments later, he was discovered heaving the knight to his feet:

Percival wanted the man's armor and had not the faintest idea how to remove it. He thought armor and body might be all of a piece and planned to put the whole carcass on a fire, in hopes that the steely carapace alone would survive the flames.

Arthur's companions took Percival into their company after that and attempted to civilize him. And indeed, he became a brilliant fighter. He even acquired a certain veneer of knightly grace.

But he remained a man of sublime simplicity, and perhaps because of this – and of his blood and his bravery – he was one of the first of the Round Table to find the Grail. It took him months of traveling, but at last he arrived at the battered castle. He hailed a guard and was admitted.

As Lancelot before him, he was welcomed to the hall. As Lancelot had, he spoke with the ailing King. He gaped at the courtiers. He gaped at the ceremony of the Grail Castle: When the page and maiden, faces still with cosmic sorrow, bore in the bleeding spear and the Grail itself, he stood like a stone. The talisman was uncovered. Its light surpassed the brightness of the sun, yet a man could gaze upon it without dazzlement or harm, and when he gazed he looked into eternity.

## Galahad at the maidens' castle

In the midst of his quest, Galahad performed a brave and kindly deed. By the River Severn, he found a castle where – for their private pleasure – seven coarse and lecherous knights had imprisoned a number of maidens. Singlehanded and without taking a life, Galahad drove the villains into the wilderness and freed the women. He gave the castle into the keeping of the highest-ranking maiden and, to ensure the women's safety, summoned all the warriors of the countryside to pay her fealty.

Then Galahad went on his way. As for the evil knights wandering the wilderness, they had the misfortune to encounter Sir Gawain and his brother, who slew them one and all.

The page and maiden left, bearing their mysterious treasures away. Percival looked at the company around him. Each one of them regarded him steadily; each one's eyes were bright with appeal. Percival opened his mouth to speak.

He closed it again. He had been warned by King Arthur's knights and courtiers about boorish chattering and unseemly curiosity. The light shivered one moment longer, and then a sigh swept through the room. Percival was led away to a bedchamber. As he passed by his hosts, the people turned their backs to him.

He was dismayed, but being Percival, he did not ask himself the reason. He retired meekly to bed and fell instantly asleep, like the creature of clear conscience that he was.

When he awoke, he called for a servant. None came. He walked out in search of his hosts, but the castle was empty. Morning mist curled coldly through the broken windows and lingered in the corridors. He walked through the mist and out the gate and across the moat to the water's edge, where he found his horse waiting. Percival armed himself and mounted and looked at the gate: It slammed shut, locking him out of the enchanted place.

But he would find the Grail once more when the time came. As for his companions, they scattered through Britain and, in their efforts to reach the Waste Land, braved the dangers that still lurked in the forests and mountains of the island. The paths seemed to shift: The ways were rocky and thronged with enemies such as they had fought in their youth—knights without names, dragons and giants.

The tales of the last quest are numerous and could while away many evenings, yet the story of the last quest of Arthur's knights can be told in a trice:

Most of the men fell out early in the chase, killed or wounded or—unlike Percival—frustrated by defeat. Gawain, Bors, Ector, Lancelot, Lionel and Percival, with the help of guides who appeared in their various paths, found their way to the fringes of the Waste Land. Lionel went mad; Ector turned back at the last. Gawain reached the Grail Castle, and Lancelot rode with him, hoping that on this second venture he would glimpse the heart of the mystery.

But Lancelot was flawed and did not see the Grail: Great though he was, his betrayal of King Arthur robbed him of this vision of the elder magic. The light that shone from the vessel left him unconscious. Gawain, bright and brave and gentlehearted, the most loyal of friends, the fiercest of enemies, saw what Lancelot was barred from seeing—the Grail itself, shining like the sun.

He asked a question: He did not ask the whole question, yet still he asked. "In the name of God," he said, when the Grail and lance had passed from the room, "tell me the meaning of these things."

The Grail, ancient in itself, was bound by some forgotten ritual; some ordering of words, long lost, controlled its antique powers. Only a man of perfect valor could speak the words, it seemed; and he had to find the perfect words. Lancelot, on his first approach to

For part of the Quest, brave Sir Gawain rode with Sir Ector de Maris, until, at a ruined chapel in a wood, a vision of failure came to both men. Sir Ector bowed to fate and turned for home. Sir Gawain, however, was more determined: Steadfastly, he journeyed on.

Alone among the knights who quested for the Grail, Galahad gazed
upon the heart of the mystery at last. The vision he found within the Grail
transported him to the realms of gold, far from the world of mortal men.

*Many knights died or failed the Grail Quest, but Lancelot's fate was the saddest:*
*He gained the Grail Castle, but his flawed honor denied him the final truth, and he*
*was left outcast while his companion, Gawain, was permitted a glimpse of the Grail.*

the magic vessel, had not spoken. Perhaps the flaw in his honor restrained his tongue. Percival had had a glimpse of the mystery. Awe-stricken, he had not spoken. But Gawain spoke. And in the asking of that honest, simple question, he unwittingly inaugurated the healing of the Waste Land. King Pellam still lay sorely wounded, but when Lancelot and Gawain rode away, they saw that the dreaded expanses of rocky aridity had been washed by recent rain; they saw tiny green shoots of new plants straining up from the dusty earth.

But others were coming to the Grail Castle then. Long leagues away, in an inlet where the gray tide washed the shores of Britain, three of Arthur's knights met to make the last venture of the Quest. All three were fatigued and battered from months of riding and from fighting the dark creatures clustered in their track. The knights were these: Sir Bors, the faithful; Sir Percival, shining with his peculiar innocence; and Galahad, cool and controlled as ever, but bright-eyed now. The end he had been formed for was in sight.

In the inlet, bobbing on the waves, was a small boat with sails of silk, rigged and ready. Not one of the men knew how it was provided. They left their horses at the shore and, without speaking, climbed into the vessel. The boat sailed itself; and accepting of any adventure, as they had been trained, the three knights gave themselves obediently to its course.

The boat took them to a rocky shore some way up the coast, where parched trees and blowing sand told the men that they had found the place they sought. A day of patient walking brought them to the Grail Castle. The drawbridge across the empty lake was down for them, and the heavy gates were standing open.

They entered together. They found King Pellam, and he made the signal that summoned the Grail, carried now by a maiden that Galahad did not know. His mother was dead.

The eyes of the company were fixed on the knights. Only Galahad spoke.

"What is the Grail and whom does it serve?"

He had found, it seemed, the exact and ancient formula that called forth the power of the Grail. Somewhere in the depths of the building, a bell rang, cool and silver-sounding. In the silence that followed, the company heard an unfamiliar sound: the hissing of a steady rain. The old King nodded and signaled to Galahad, who took the spear from the page who bore it and dipped his own hand in the blood. He touched the King's forehead with his bloody hand and stepped back.

And the King rose to his feet again, strong as in youth, a whole man now. He signaled to Galahad his grandson and to Percival his nephew.

To Percival he said, "You will guard the Grail now." He took the Grail from the Grail Maiden and placed the maiden's hand in the knight's.

To Galahad he said, "Your quest is done and you shall have your answer."

Then King Pellam lifted the Grail and signaled to Galahad that he should look into its depths.

Galahad peered down into the golden hemisphere; sunlight glittered on his face. A curious expression crossed it as he contemplated the depths of the Grail — of fear and horror, of joy and power too great for mortals. He died where he stood, and the King caught him as he fell.

And over his bright head, the Grail King spoke to Sir Bors.

"You are the messenger," he said. "Return to your King and tell him this: Tell him that the Quest for the Grail is finished and the land restored again. Tell him that the greatest deeds are done and that a time of endings follows swiftly."

And Sir Bors obeyed the Grail King's order. He alone returned to Camelot. He arrived on a winter's night, while the wind howled around him, and in the bright hall he found those of his comrades who had survived the Quest — Lancelot and Gawain were there, with Bedevere, Gareth and Gaheris.

When he had been fed and bathed and had warmed himself beside the fire, Sir Bors told the company the story of the Grail. And when he had finished, he said the words of the Grail King — that the time of endings was coming.

And that was true. The fall of Camelot and that long, dark grief was almost upon King Arthur. The King did not speak, but he nodded sadly. When he had passed and his kingdom had fallen, the glory of the valiant would pass from the earth.

# The Great King's Last Battle

The fellowship of the Round Table was undone on a fine day in May, when King Arthur was old and tired and his court rife with secret factions. The King and his champion, Lancelot, had enemies in the court, and chief among them was Mordred, Arthur's bastard son. Mordred had four half brothers: Agravain, as spiteful as Mordred himself; and Gawain, Gaheris and Gareth, steadfastly faithful to Lancelot and the King. When Mordred and Agravain made their move, their brothers flatly refused to join in it.

Mordred was determined to show that Lancelot was the Queen's lover and thus a traitor to his King. One night, therefore, Mordred and Agravain—with twelve companion knights—armed themselves and stole up the winding stair that led to the Queen's chamber. They pounded on the door. Lancelot answered. He was indeed with the Queen—long his lover—and unarmed. But the knights could not press their advantage, crowded as they were on the shadowy stair. Lancelot opened the door; he pulled the first knight, who was Colgrevaunce, into the chamber and slammed the door again. While the Queen watched, he killed Colgrevaunce with the man's own sword. Then, in Colegrevaunce's armor, he hacked his way down the stair, slaughtering all the conspirators except Mordred the talebearer, who fled.

*Through the treachery of Mordred, King Arthur's bastard son, Queen Guinevere was doomed to die by fire; it was Sir Lancelot who rescued her.*

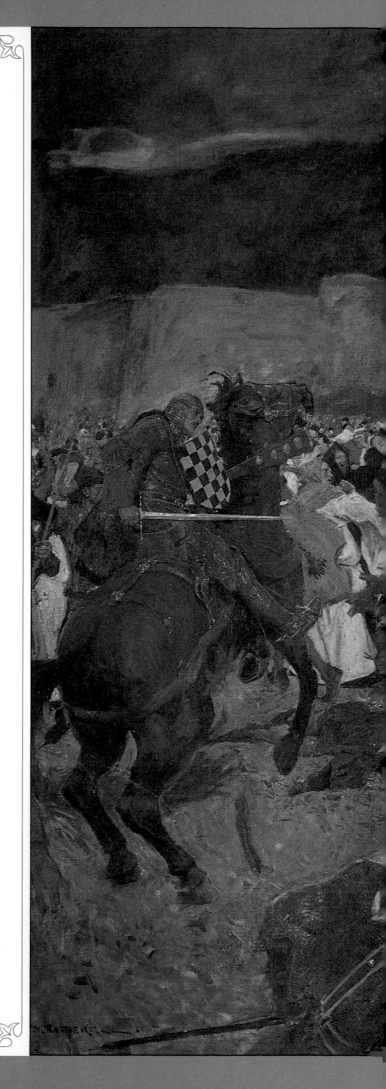

Lancelot and his supporters retreated to his own fortress, Joyous Garde. Mordred went to the King with his story. And Arthur, trapped by the law he himself had made, condemned his wife Guinevere to burn for her infidelity, although it grieved him and his own knights bitterly protested.

But in the gray dawn of the execution morning, when Guinevere was bound to the stake, Lancelot and his men charged through the throng to rescue the Queen. In the fight to reach her, Lancelot struck out blindly and, all unknowing, killed Gareth and Gaheris, both unarmed. He freed the Queen and set her on his own horse, and took her to his fortress.

When he heard of the slaying of his brothers, Gawain wept. And although he was Lancelot's friend—and staunchest supporter against Mordred's intrigues—he swore revenge. With Arthur's armies Gawain laid siege to Joyous Garde and called upon Lancelot to meet him in single combat—the custom since the earliest age of heroes. But Lancelot refused to fight Gawain or the King, for he loved them. He withstood the siege for months, until men of the Church persuaded Arthur to take Guinevere back. She went; it was her duty. Lancelot and Guinevere said their farewells then. Lancelot and his company went in exile to his lands in France.

The fellowship was broken, the bright honor of the Round Table stained. Arthur and his company returned to silent Camelot, and Arthur waited for the final act.

Gawain brought it about; he insisted that Arthur's honor be avenged. And at last, with Gawain at the head of his army, Arthur traveled to France to battle Lancelot. He left his son, Mordred, as regent in England.

For months the armies fought in France, until Lancelot's land was laid waste. Each day, Gawain challenged his old friend to sin-

*This was the battle that ended King Arthur's glory: his spear through the body of his son, the son's sword dealing the father the death blow.*

gle combat, and each day Lancelot refused, until Gawain called down scorn upon his honor. Lancelot agreed to fight.

They met in the field before Lancelot's fortress gates. All the morning Gawain's strength waxed, and Lancelot, well aware of the uncanny power that was in his friend and enemy, husbanded his strength. When noon came, they fought on, but Gawain's strength gradually waned, until it was like that of other mortals, and Lancelot found the opening to strike Sir Gawain down.

Gawain lay in the dust, bright blood pouring from his broken skull, and implored Lancelot to finish him. But Lancelot refused. "It goes against my honor to strike a man I have felled," he said. "When you can stand, I will fight you again." And he turned and left.

So an uneasy truce was kept while Gawain healed. He met Lancelot again to fight, and again Lancelot gave way in the morning and triumphed in the afternoon. Again his sword cleaved Gawain's skull, and again the blood poured onto the ground. Gawain had been felled, yet Lancelot would not strike his old companion where he lay.

They were not fated to fight again, however, for word reached them of Mordred the traitor, who had usurped the throne. He had tried, too, to marry Guinevere—his father's wife; it was she who sent appeals for help.

Then Arthur swore to kill his son, and sailed for home. The armies met on Salisbury Plain; the flower of chivalry died that day. And as he had sworn, Arthur found Mordred and put his spear through the author of his grief. But Mordred did not die at once. Howling like an animal, he thrust himself forward on the spear until his belly met the handguard, and with his broadsword he struck his father's head, through helmet and hair and bone to brain. Then Mordred fell.

*Attended by his faithful knight Sir Bedevere, the dying King awaited the enchanted barge that would bear him across the waters to another world.*

Arthur sank to the ground. The battle-field was still, save for the moans of the wounded and the scrabbling of the looters who crept among the bodies. The King closed his eyes a moment, fighting for consciousness, for he had something left to do. When he opened them he saw a faithful face: Sir Bedevere, one of the few companions left alive, bent over him and whispered his name.

King Arthur commanded Bedevere to take the last action: His sword, Excalibur, must be returned to the waters whence it had come and to the people of the other world who had made the great blade. There was a lake near the field, still and mist-shrouded, and into this lake the reluctant Bedevere threw the sword. It did not strike the water: A hand broke the surface and seized Excalibur in the air. Without a ripple, hand and sword vanished.

It was said that Bedevere carried the King to the lake edge then, and both watched as a silk-draped boat glided through the mist. In the boat were tall women sheathed in black; they took the wounded King into their arms and glided away over the water with him, and Bedevere wept to see the end.

He thought—and others thought—that Arthur had not died. The women, it was said, were the company of the enchantress Morgan le Fay, who took Arthur to the Isle of Apples, Avalon, to heal and protect him until England should need him again.

And as for Guinevere, she retired to a nunnery, where she died. Lancelot, it was said, went into the wilderness, where he, too, died. And Bedevere and the few knights who had survived scattered, to journey forever alone in foreign lands. When they were old, they told the tales of their youth and of the shining fellowship they once had, when Arthur ruled Britain and true men fought with the honor of the valiant.

*It is said that Arthur, the once and future King, sleeps still in the fairy isle of Avalon, waiting for the day when his people will call for him again.*

# Acknowledgments

The editors are particularly indebted to John Dorst, consultant, for his help in the preparation of this volume. The editors also wish to thank the following persons and institutions: François Avril, Curator, Département des Manuscrits, Bibliothèque Nationale, Paris; Alasdair Auld, Director, Glasgow Art Gallery and Museum; Marimar Benítez, Museo de Arte de Ponce, Ponce, Puerto Rico; William Buchanan, Glasgow College of Art; Jean-Loup Charmet, Paris; Elizabeth Cumming, Keeper of Fine Art Collections, Edinburgh City Museums and Art Galleries; Michael Cuthbert, The Edinburgh College of Art; Giuseppe Dondi, Director, Biblioteca Nazionale, Turin; Lindsay Errington, Assistant Keeper, National Gallery of Scotland, Edinburgh; Henry Ford, Jeremy Maas Gallery, London; Martin Forrest, Bourne Fine Art Ltd., Edinburgh; Marielise Göpel, Archiv für Kunst und Geschichte, West Berlin; Claus Hansmann, Stockdorf, Germany; Jennifer Harris, Assistant Keeper, Whitworth Art Gallery, Manchester, England; Gill Hedley, Keeper of Art, Southampton Art Gallery, England; Heidi Klein, Bildarchiv Preussischer Kulturbesitz, Bonn; Kunsthistorisches Institut, Bonn; Graham Langton, Publications, Tate Gallery, London; Martin Lee, Harrap Ltd., London; Françoise Lemonnier, Bibliothèque Nationale, Paris; Stefania Rossi Minutelli, Biblioteca Marciana, Venice; Gianalbino Ravalli Modoni, Director, Biblioteca Marciana, Venice; Alice Munro-Faure, Sotheby Parke Bernet & Co., London; Joseph Natanson, Rome; Maureen Park, Assistant Keeper, Glasgow Art Gallery and Museum; Christine Poulson, London; Michel Rival, Bibliothèque Nationale, Paris; Royal Library, Copenhagen; R. A. Saunders, Deputy Curator and Keeper of Art, Paisley Art Gallery, Scotland; Justin Schiller, New York City; Joseph Setchell, King Arthur's Hall Ltd., Tintagel, England; Tessa Sidey, Assistant Keeper, Birmingham Museum and Art Gallery, England; Peyton Skipwith, Fine Art Society, London; Soviet Copyright Agency, Moscow; Konrad Vanja, Director, Museum für Deutsche Volkskunde SMPQ, West Berlin; Frédéric Vergne, Librarian, Musée Condé, Chantilly, France; Alessandro Vitale, Biblioteca Nazionale, Turin; Clara Young, Keeper of Art, Dundee Museums and Art Galleries, Scotland.

# Picture Credits

# Bibliography

Barber, Richard:
*King Arthur in Legend and History*. Ipswich, England: The Boydell Press, 1973.
*The Knight and Chivalry*. New York: Harper & Row, 1982.
*Book of British Birds*. London: Drive Publications, 1974.
Brombert, Victor, ed., *The Hero in Literature*. Greenwich, Connecticut: Fawcett, 1969.
*Castles*. New York: Greenwich House, 1982.
Cavendish, Richard, *King Arthur & The Grail: The Arthurian Legends and Their Meaning*. New York: Taplinger, 1979.*
Coolidge, Olivia E., *Legends of the North*. Boston: Houghton Mifflin, 1951.
Cross, Tom Peete, and Clark Harris Slover, eds., *Ancient Irish Tales*. Totowa, New Jersey: Barnes & Noble, 1969.*
Cunliffe, Barry, *The Celtic World*. New York: McGraw-Hill, 1979.
Cutler, U. Waldo, *Stories of King Arthur and His Knights*. New York: Thomas Y. Crowell, 1924.
De Vries, Jan, *Heroic Song and Heroic Legend*. Transl. by B. J. Timmer. New York: Arno Press, 1978 (reprint).
Dillon, Myles, *Early Irish Literature*.

The University of Chicago Press, 1972 (reprint).*
Gantz, Jeffrey, transl.:
*Early Irish Myths and Sagas*. New York: Penguin Books, 1982.*
*The Mabinogion*. New York: Penguin Books, 1981.
Gibson, Michael, *The Knights*. New York: Arco Publishing, 1981.
Goodrich, Norma Lorre, *Medieval Myths*. New York: New American Library, 1977.
Green, Roger Lancelyn, *King Arthur and His Knights of the Round Table: Newly Re-Told Out of the Old Romances*. Harmondsworth, England: Puffin Books, 1982.
Gregory, Lady, ed. and transl.:
*Cuchulain of Muirthemne: The Story of the Men of the Red Branch of Ulster*. Gerrards Cross, England: Colin Smythe, 1979 (reprint of 1902 edition).*
*Gods and Fighting Men: The Story of the Tuatha De Danaan and of the Fianna of Ireland*. Gerrards Cross, England: Colin Smythe, 1979 (reprint of 1904 edition).*
Hamilton, Edith, *Mythology*. New York: New American Library, 1969 (reprint).
Heller, Julek, and Deirdre Headon, *Knights*. New York: Schocken Books, 1982.

Holmes, Urban Tigner, *Chrétien de Troyes*. New York: Twayne Publishers, 1970.
Hull, Eleanor, ed. and compiler, *The Cuchullin Saga in Irish Literature*. London: David Nutt in the Strand, 1898.
Hyde, Douglas, *A Literary History of Ireland*. London: Ernest Benn, 1969.
Jackson, Kenneth Hurlstone, transl., *A Celtic Miscellany: Translations from the Celtic Literatures*. London: Routledge & Kegan Paul, 1951.
Jenkins, Elizabeth, *The Mystery of King Arthur*. New York: Coward, McCann & Geoghegan, 1975.
Jiriczek, Otto L., *Northern Hero Legends*. London: J. M. Dent, 1902.
Jones, Gwyn, *Scandinavian Legends and Folk-tales*. London: Oxford University Press, 1956.
Joyce, P. W., *A Smaller Social History of Ancient Ireland*. London: Longmans, Green, 1906.*
Ker, W. P., *Epic and Romance: Essays on Medieval Literature*. New York: Dover Publications, 1957.
Kinsella, Thomas, transl., *The Tain*. London: Oxford University Press, 1970.*
Knowles, Sir James, compiler, *King Arthur and His Knights*. New York:

Harper & Brothers, 1923.

Leach, Maria, ed., *Funk & Wagnalls Standard Dictionary of Folklore, Mythology and Legend.* 2 vols. New York: Funk & Wagnalls, 1949.*

Lowry, Shirley Park, *Familiar Mysteries: The Truth in Myth.* New York: Oxford University Press, 1982.

MacKenzie, Donald A., *Teutonic Myth and Legend.* Boston: Longwood Press, 1978 (reprint of 1934 edition).

MacManus, Seumas, *The Story of the Irish Race: A Popular History of Ireland.* Old Greenwich, Connecticut: The Devin-Adair Co., 1983.*

Malory, Sir Thomas:
*Le Morte D'Arthur.* 2 vols. Edited by Janet Cowen. New York: Penguin Books, 1983.
*Le Morte Darthur.* Edited by R. M. Lumiansky. New York: Charles Scribner's Sons, 1982.*
*Tales of King Arthur.* Edited by Michael Senior. New York: Schocken Books, 1980.*

Matarasso, P. M., transl., *The Quest of the Holy Grail.* New York: Penguin Books, 1982.

Matthews, John, *The Grail: Quest for the Eternal.* New York: Crossroad Publishing, 1981.

*Medieval Epics.* New York: The Modern Library, 1963.*

Nutt, Alfred, *Studies on the Legend of the Holy Grail with Especial Reference to the Hypothesis of Its Celtic Origin.* New York: Cooper Square, 1965.

Oinas, Felix J., ed., *Heroic Epic and Saga: An Introduction to the World's Great Folk Epics.* Bloomington: Indiana University Press, 1978.

Pyle, Howard, *The Story of the Champions of the Round Table.* New York: Dover Publications, 1968 (reprint of 1905 edition).

Rees, Alwyn and Brinley, *Celtic Heritage: Ancient Tradition in Ireland and Wales.* New York: Thames and Hudson, 1961.*

Rolleston, T. W., *The High Deeds of Finn and Other Bardic Romances of Ancient Ireland.* New York: Lemma Publishing, 1973.

Ross, Anne, *Pagan Celtic Britain: Studies in Iconography and Tradition.* London: Routledge and Kegan Paul, 1967.

Sayers, Dorothy L., transl., *The Song of Roland.* New York: Penguin Books, 1981 (reprint).

Sophocles, *The Oedipus Cycle.* Transl. by Dudley Fitts and Robert Fitzgerald. New York: Harcourt, Brace & World, 1949.

Squire, Charles, *Celtic Myth & Legend: Poetry & Romance.* North Hollywood, California: Newcastle Publishing, 1975 (reprint of 1905 edition).

Stephens, James, *Irish Fairy Tales.* New York: Abaris Books, 1978.

Sutcliff, Rosemary:
*The High Deeds of Finn Mac Cool.* New York: E. P. Dutton, 1967.
*The Hound of Ulster.* New York: E. P. Dutton, 1963.

Troyes, Chrétien de, *Arthurian Romances.* Transl. by W. Wistar Comfort. New York: E. P. Dutton, 1913.*

Weston, Jessie L., *From Ritual to Romance.* New York: Anchor Books, 1957 (reprint of 1920 edition).

*Titles marked with an asterisk were especially helpful in the preparation of this volume.*

## The Author

Brendan Lehane was born in London of
Irish parents. A graduate of Cambridge
University, he was a magazine journal-
ist before launching a career as an au-
thor. His books include *The Companion
Guide to Ireland, The Complete Flea, The
Quest of Three Abbots* and *The Power of
Plants.* For Time-Life Books he has writ-
ten *Dublin* in The Great Cities series,
*The Northwest Passage* in The Seafarers
series, and *Wizards and Witches* in The
Enchanted World series.

## Chief Series Consultant

Tristram Potter Coffin, Professor of
English at the University of Pennsylva-
nia, is a leading authority on folklore.
He is the author or editor of numerous
books and more than one hundred arti-
cles. His best-known works are *The British Traditional Ballad in North America, The
Old Ball Game, The Book of Christmas Folklore* and *The Female Hero.*

This volume is one of a series that is based
on myths, legends and folk tales.

*Other Publications:*

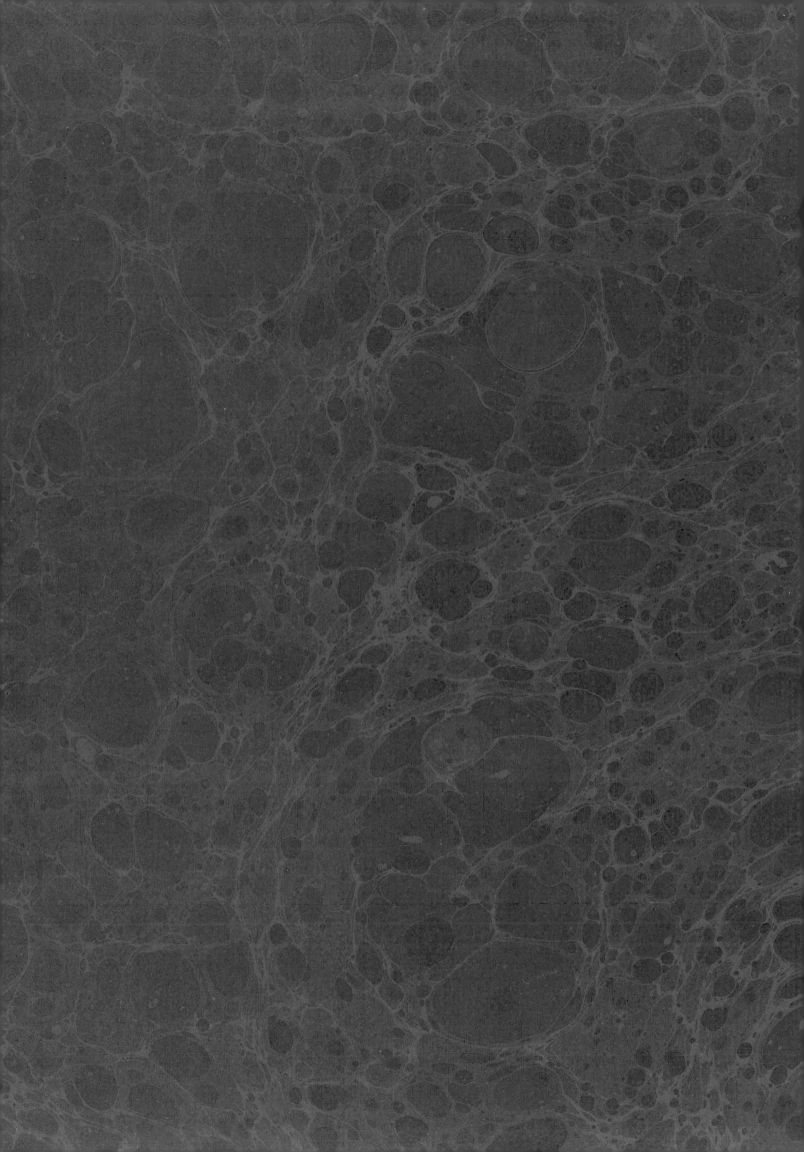